THE MUSKETEERS—
TWENTY YEARS LATER

Borgo Press Books Edited & Translated by FRANK J. MORLOCK

Alcestis: A Play in Five Acts, by Philippe Quinault * Anna Karenina: A Play in Five Acts, by Edmond Guiraud, from Leo Tolstoy * Anthony: A Play in Five Acts, by Alexandre Dumas, Père * Atys: A Play in Five Acts, by Philippe Quinault * The Boss Lady: A Play in Five Acts, by Paul Féval, Père * The Children of Captain Grant: A Play in Five Acts, by Jules Verne & Adolphe d'Ennery * Cleopatra: A Play in Five Acts, by Victorien Sardou * Crime and Punishment: A Play in Three Acts, by Frank J. Morlock, from Fyodor Dostoyevsky * Don Quixote: A Play in Three Acts, by Victorien Sardou, from Miguel de Cervantes * The Dream of a Summer Night: A Fantasy Play in Three Acts, by Paul Meurice * Falstaff: A Play in Four Acts, by William Shakespeare, John Dennis, William Kendrick, & Frank J. Morlock * The Idiot: A Play in Three Acts, by Frank J. Morlock, from Fyodor Dostoyevsky * Isis: A Play in Five Acts, by Philippe Quinault * Jesus of Nazareth: A Play in Three Acts, by Paul Demasy * The Jew of Venice: A Play in Five Acts, by Ferdinand Dugué * Joan of Arc: A Play in Five Acts, by Charles Desnoyer * The Lily of the Valley: A Play in Five Acts, by Théodore Barrière & Arthur de Beauplan, from Honoré de Balzac * Lord Byron in Venice: A Play in Three Acts, by Jacques Ancelot * Louis XIV and the Affair of the Poisons: A Play in Five Acts, by Victorien Sardou * The Man Who Saw the Devil: A Play in Two Acts, by Gaston Leroux * Mathias Sandorf: A Play in Three Acts, by Jules Verne & William Busnach * Michael Strogoff: A Play in Five Acts, by Jules Verne & Adolphe d'Ennery * Les Misérables: A Play in Two Acts, by Victor Hugo, Paul Meurice, & Charles Victor Hugo * Monte Cristo, Part One: A Play in Five Acts, by Alexandre Dumas, Père * Monte Cristo, Part Two: A Play in Five Acts, by Alexandre Dumas, Père * Monte Cristo, Part Three: A Play in Five Acts, by Alexandre Dumas, Père * Monte Cristo, Part Four: A Play in Five Acts, by Alexandre Dumas, Père * The Musketeers—Twenty Years Later: A Play in Five Acts, by Alexandre Dumas, Père * The Mysteries of Paris: A Play in Five Acts, by Eugène Sue & Prosper Dinaux * Napoléon Bonaparte: A Play in Six Acts, by Alexandre Dumas, Père * Ninety-Three: A Play in Four Acts, by Victor Hugo & Paul Meurice * Notes from the Underground: A Play in Two Acts, by Frank J. Morlock, from Fyodor Dostoyevsky * Outrageous Women: Lady MacBeth and Other French Plays, edited by Frank J. Morlock * Peau de Chagrin: A Play in Five Acts, by Louis Judicis, from Honoré de Balzac * The Prisoner of the Bastille: A Play in Five Acts, by Alexandre Dumas, Père * A Raw Youth: A Play in Five Acts, by Frank J. Morlock, from Fyodor Dostoyevsky * Richard Darlington: A Play in Three Acts, by Alexandre Dumas, Père * The San Felice: A Play in Five Acts, by Maurice Drack, from Alexander Dumas, Père * Saul and David: A Play in Five Acts, by Voltaire * Shylock, the Merchant of Venice: A Play in Three Acts, by Alfred de Vigny * Socrates: A Play in Three Acts, by Voltaire * The Son of Porthos: A Play in Five Acts, by Émile Blavet, from M. Paul Mahalin * The Stendhal Hamlet Scenarios and Other Shakespearean Shorts from the French, edited by Frank J. Morlock * A Summer Night's Dream: A Play in Three Acts, by Joseph-Bernard Rosier & Adolphe de Leuwen * The Three Musketeers: A Play in Five Acts, by Alexandre Dumas, Père * Urbain Grandier and the Devils of Loudon: A Play in Four Acts, by Alexandre Dumas, Père * The Voyage Through the Impossible: A Play in Three Acts, by Jules Verne & Adolphe d'Ennery * The Whites and the Blues: A Play in Five Acts, by Alexandre Dumas, Père * William Shakespeare: A Play in Six Acts, by Ferdinand Dugué

THE MUSKETEERS— TWENTY YEARS LATER

A PLAY IN FIVE ACTS

by

Alexandre Dumas, Père

Translated and Adapted by Frank J. Morlock

THE BORGO PRESS

An Imprint of Wildside Press LLC

MMX

CONTENTS

DEDICATION

To

Conrad Cady

CAST OF CHARACTERS

- INNKEEPER
- UNKNOWN
- MORDAUNT
- HOSTESS
- PATAUD
- BRIGADIER
- DE WINTER
- GRIMAUD
- MADELEINE
- D'ARTAGNAN
- PORTHOS
- MOUSQUETON
- ATHOS
- ARAMIS

- TOMY

- PARRY

- QUEEN

- ANDRÉ

- BOATMAN

- GROSLOW

- CROMWELL

- SOLDIER

- FINDLEY

- SENTINEL

- KING

- SECOND SENTINEL

- SERGEANT

- TOM LOWE

- CLERK

- BLAISOIS

PROLOGUE

The Inn of Pernes near Bethune. A door at the front to the right. A stairway in the back. At the left, a window and a door to the hôtel.

(An unknown seated at a table. The host, hostess.)

INNKEEPER

What would you like?

UNKNOWN

Some bread and wine first, if you please—for I haven't had anything since morning.

INNKEEPER

We'll give you that.

(Innkeeper opens the door to the cellar. The Hostess appears at the head of the stairs.)

HOSTESS

Eh! Man!

INNKEEPER

What?

HOSTESS

The monk's mule.

INNKEEPER

(going down)

Good.

HOSTESS

Right away.

INNKEEPER

(from the depth of the cellar)

Ah, yes, right away. As though they paid well your Mendicant monks.

HOSTESS

This one pays—he pays in gold even!

(Innkeeper reappears with a bottle in his hand.)

INNKEEPER

Bah! In that case it's another matter.

(he puts the bottle on the table and opens the window of the court-yard)

Hey! Pataud!

VOICE

What is it?

INNKEEPER

The mule for his Reverence—right away.

UNKNOWN

You have a monk with you?

INNKEEPER

Yes.

UNKNOWN

Of what denomination?

INNKEEPER

Is there such a thing as an order of questioners?

UNKNOWN

I don't think so.

INNKEEPER

I'm angry—this one would be surely.

UNKNOWN

He asks you many questions?

INNKEEPER

Lord God! He's done nothing but since he arrived. "How many people are there here in Bethune? Have you ever been in an Augustine convent?" They say one of his relatives lost something there. It's been a dozen years he's been looking for what he lost.

(Someone knocks at the window giving on the high way.)

VOICE

Hey, friend!

HOSTESS

Wait—someone's knocking over there.

INNKEEPER

Some people on horseback. If they were Spanish—

HOSTESS

Oh, no—since they speak French.

VOICE

Friend—friend….

(outside)

INNKEEPER

(opening)

What do you want, Brigadier?

BRIGADIER

Can you give me news of the Spanish army?

(He enters by the door at the left followed by some men.)

INNKEEPER

Ah—damn—all the world can tell you. The plunderers. You cannot go a hundred steps without meeting them.

BRIGADIER

Some partisans, yes—but it is the regular army we are looking for.

(Mordaunt dressed in the robe of a monk appears at the top of the stairs, stops and listens.)

INNKEEPER

Ah! The army is another matter.

BRIGADIER

Listen. We've been sent by M. Le Prune. The Spanish Army has left its cantonments and we are not sure where it is. Fifty patrols are en route at this moment—and there's a hundred pistoles to whoever can give exact news of the enemy's whereabouts.

UNKNOWN

I can give you that.

BRIGADIER

You?

UNKNOWN

Yes, me.

BRIGADIER

You know where the Spanish Army is?

UNKNOWN

I do. It crossed the Lys River yesterday.

BRIGADIER

Where?

UNKNOWN

Between Saint Venant and Aire.

BRIGADIER

By whom is it commanded?

UNKNOWN

By the Archduke in person.

BRIGADIER

How many men is it made up of?

UNKNOWN

Eighteen thousand men.

BRIGADIER

And it's marching on?

UNKNOWN

On Lens.

BRIGADIER

How do you know these details?

UNKNOWN

I was returning from Hazebrouch to Bethune when the Spaniards captured me and forced me to serve as their guide. Three leagues from here, thanks to the darkness, I escaped.

BRIGADIER

And can we rely on the statements you have given?

UNKNOWN

As if you had seen them yourself, I tell you.

BRIGADIER

Your name?

UNKNOWN

Why?

BRIGADIER

To send you the promised reward, if your observations are exact.

UNKNOWN

Useless.

BRIGADIER

Why useless?

UNKNOWN

One speaks the truth for nothing—One lies for money. I've spoken the truth—you owe me nothing.

BRIGADIER

Still, my friend, since 100 pistoles have been promised by M. Le Prune.

UNKNOWN

If I've told the truth, you will send the hundred pistoles to the Cure of Bethune who will distribute them to the poor.

BRIGADIER

But we will drink a glass of wine together—to the health of our general and to France.

UNKNOWN

Thanks! Better not.

BRIGADIER

Why's that?

UNKNOWN

Because, you don't know me, and if one day, you should chance to know me, you might repent of having touched your glass to mine. Follow your route sir, and haste to bring the news I have given you to your general.

BRIGADIER

You are right. Your hand, my friend!

UNKNOWN

(recoiling)

It would be too much honor for me.

BRIGADIER

Singular personality

(to his men)

Come on—en route!

(he leaves)

MORDAUNT

(aside)

Yes-singular personality. Yet, he lives in Bethune, as he said. Perhaps, through him, I will have some intelligence.

(Coming down and sitting at a table.)

HOSTESS

What do you want, my reverend?

MORDAUNT

A lamp—that's all! I already asked for my mule.

HOSTESS

He's already coming.

MORDAUNT

Thanks.

(to Unknown)

You are from around here, Sir?

UNKNOWN

I am from Bethune.

MORDAUNT

Ah—from Bethune—and you lived in Bethune for a long time?

UNKNOWN

I was born here.

MORDAUNT

(to the Hostess who brings a lamp)

Thanks!

(he opens a geographic map—to the unknown)

Sir, how far are we from Bethune to Lilliers?

UNKNOWN

Three leagues.

MORDAUNT

And from Bethune to Armentiers?

UNKNOWN

Seven.

MORDAUNT

Have you sometimes taken that route?

UNKNOWN

Often.

MORDAUNT

Is it very dangerous?

UNKNOWN

In what respect?

MORDAUNT

In respect that one can be assassinated?

UNKNOWN

At least it isn't in time of war—as today, for example, the route is very secure.

MORDAUNT

Safe!

(aside)

I have indeed thought it—it must be some special vengeance. Ah, at my return, I will pass this way again—I've spent enough time on the business of Mr. Cromwell so I can do a bit of my own—

(aloud)

Now sir, could you tell me—

(Enter de Winter and the Innkeeper.)

DE WINTER

(to Innkeeper)

Speak then, Master!

INNKEEPER

There, your Lordship!

MORDAUNT

(raising his head)

Oh! Oh!

DE WINTER

Where am I here if you please?

INNKEEPER

At Pernes, Sir.

MORDAUNT

(aside)

It's him. I didn't think he was in France.

DE WINTER

At Pernes between Lilliers and Saint-Pol then?

INNKEEPER

Exactly.

DE WINTER

That's fine.

INNKEEPER

Your Lordship desires that someone serve him supper?

DE WINTER

No—I only want to get some information about the way—

MORDAUNT

(aside)

More I watch him, the more I hear him—the more this face and voice—

INNKEEPER

Some information about the way—at your service, sir.

DE WINTER

To go to Doulens—which is the road one must take?

INNKEEPER

That to Paris.

DE WINTER

Then one has only to follow it to the right?

INNKEEPER

But this road is infested with Spanish partisans. I don't advise you to take it, or if you take it, go by day.

DE WINTER

Impossible—I must continue on my way.

INNKEEPER

Then take the back road.

DE WINTER

But won't I get lost?

INNKEEPER

Ah—damn—at night.

DE WINTER

My friend, would you serve me as a guide.

HOSTESS

(approaching)

Oh no, sir!

(to her husband)

I really hope you won't accept.

DE WINTER

Why my good woman—I will give a reward.

HOSTESS

No, sir, for all the gold in the world I won't let him go so someone can kill him.

DE WINTER

And who would do that?

HOSTESS

Who would do it? The Spanish Brigands, of course.

DE WINTER

My friend—here are twenty pistoles for whoever will act as my guide.

INNKEEPER

If it were forty, sir, if it were a hundred, I would refuse. You see, there are things more precious in the world and that's life—and to chance it at this hour in this country, in the midst of all these bandits, it's to stake one's life on a roll of the dice.

DE WINTER

My friend, if money doesn't tempt you—let me speak to you in the name of humanity—in serving as my guide—in aiding me to get to Paris as soon as possible, you will render an immense service to someone who is in danger of death.

UNKNOWN

(rising)

If it would be such a great service as you say, sir—and you wish to accept me as your guide—here I am.

DE WINTER

You.

UNKNOWN

Yes, me. Do you accept, sir?

DE WINTER

Certainly—and in your turn, here—my friend.

(wishing to give him a purse)

UNKNOWN

Pardon, sir, I said if there was a service to perform—and not money to be gained.

DE WINTER

Then, sir—

UNKNOWN

Each makes his conditions—these are mine.

DE WINTER

(aside)

This is singular. It seems to me I've seen this man before.

UNKNOWN

(aside)

I am not deceived. It is indeed him.

DE WINTER

(to Innkeeper)

Now, my friend, here's a guinea. Do exactly what I tell you to do.

INNKEEPER

Speak, sir.

DE WINTER

A man is waiting for me at Doulens at the Lis Couronne; but as I am late, it is possible that this man, having tired waiting for me—is pushing on to here.

INNKEEPER

How will I recognize him?

DE WINTER

Dressed as a lackey; thirty five to forty years of age—hair and beard—black. Silent like a stone; as to the rest—he responds to the name of Grimaud.

INNKEEPER

And he will ask?

DE WINTER

He will ask for Lord de Winter.

UNKNOWN

(aside)

Indeed, it is him.

MORDAUNT

(aside)

Ah, my dear uncle, I would have thought you'd kept a stricter incognito.

INNKEEPER

What shall I say to him?

DE WINTER

I've gotten ahead of him and he will rejoin me. If he doesn't rejoin me, he will find me at Palais at my old lodging in the Palais Royale.

(to the Unknown)

Do you wish to come, my friend?

UNKNOWN

Yes, sir, and it is not the first time that I served you as guide.

DE WINTER

How's that?

UNKNOWN

Recall the night of October 22.

DE WINTER

1636?

UNKNOWN

Yes—recall the route from Bethune to Armentiers.

DE WINTER

Silence! Yes, I recognize you—come-come—

(They leave by the left. The Innkeeper goes off to the right.)

MORDAUNT

(rising, aside)

The night of October 22—the road from Bethune to Armentiers. What a strange coincidence! The 22nd of October—the day my mother died—the road from Bethune to Armentiers—the place where she disappeared. It's as if chance is doing more for me than all the other calculation and research. Come on, I must follow this man.

(aloud)

My mule! My mule!

HOSTESS

You ask?

MORDAUNT

My mule is ready?

HOSTESS

She's waiting for you at the door.

MORDAUNT

Thanks. You are paid, right?

HOSTESS

Yes—certainly. It only remains for me to ask your blessing.

MORDAUNT

(leaving)

God protect you!

HOSTESS

Pierre!

(calling)

Pierre—come on, he just left. He won't be still until he's assassinated

(gunshots far off)

Ah, my God—wait—more gun fire—Pierre!

(she opens the window)

Pataud!

VOICE

What?

HOSTESS

Have you seen your master?

VOICE

He's there in the garden.

HOSTESS

Ah—just in time!

(she turns and perceives Grimaud)

Sir.

(Grimaud bows.)

HOSTESS

From where are you come?

(Grimaud points to the door.)

HOSTESS

By the door—then you are on foot?

(Grimaud makes an affirmative sign.)

HOSTESS

Then what do you want?

(Grimaud makes a sign that he wants to drink.)

HOSTESS

I understand. You have the misfortune to be a mute, sir?

(Grimaud makes an affirmative sign.)

HOSTESS

Oh, poor dear man.

(The Innkeeper returns.)

HOSTESS

Speak, my friend—here's a fellow makes no noise—he is mute.

INNKEEPER

Mute—maybe it's our man. He resembles the description given to me.

(going to Grimaud)

Well, sir! Are you looking for someone?

(Grimaud lifts his head.)

INNKEEPER

An Englishman

(same sign)

(pause)

Who is named Lord de Winter?

GRIMAUD

Yes.

HOSTESS

Alas! The mute can speak.

INNKEEPER

And your name?

GRIMAUD

Grimaud.

INNKEEPER

Well, Mr. Grimaud, the person who was waiting for you at Doulens.

GRIMAUD

Yes.

INNKEEPER

At the Couronne.

GRIMAUD

Yes.

INNKEEPER

Just left ten minutes ago with a guide—and said to tell you to find him at Paris at his old lodgings in the Palais Royale.

GRIMAUD

Good!

INNKEEPER

Then, since your commission is finished, you will stay?

GRIMAUD

Yes.

INNKEEPER

Have you eaten?

GRIMAUD

No.

INNKEEPER

Then you will sup and sleep here?

GRIMAUD

Yes.

INNKEEPER

And will you leave?

GRIMAUD

Tomorrow.

INNKEEPER

Well—here's one who isn't talkative.

(Someone knocks at the side door.)

HOSTESS

Who is there?

PATAUD

Open, open—neighbors who bring a wounded man.

INNKEEPER

A wounded man!

UNKNOWN

It's I, it's I—open!

HOSTESS

What, this brave men—?

INNKEEPER

Who accompanied the English Lord.

HOSTESS

Well—was I right to say not to go?

INNKEEPER

A surgeon! A surgeon!

(to Grimaud)

Sir, you have a horse—you must ride to St. Pol and return with a surgeon.

GRIMAUD

How many leagues?

INNKEEPER

A league and a half!

GRIMAUD

I'm going.

(he leaves)

HOSTESS

Poor brave man—we must put him in a room.

UNKNOWN

Oh no, a mattress on this table. I suffer much.

INNKEEPER

(to wife)

Get a mattress.

(to Unknown)

What happened, sir?

UNKNOWN

Two hundred feet from here we were attacked by Spaniards, but happily nothing has happened to Lord de Winter.

(The Hostess throws a mattress from the top of the stairs.)

HOSTESS

There!

INNKEEPER

Fine—lie on that—a pillow—a cushion. What can one do for you to ease you, sir?

UNKNOWN

Nothing. The wound is mortal.

INNKEEPER

Do you need anything?

UNKNOWN

Water, I'm thirsty!

INNKEEPER

Wait.

UNKNOWN

Thanks—but can you go find me a priest?

(Mordaunt reappears at the door.)

HOSTESS

Ah, my reverend, come, come, it is the Lord you followed.

MORDAUNT

Here I am.

HOSTESS

(showing Mordaunt to the wounded man)

Sir.

UNKNOWN

Mercy—come quickly.

MORDAUNT

Let everyone leave us.

INNKEEPER

That's all right—there's a strange monk.

HOSTESS

Oh! You! You are a heretic.

(they leave)

MORDAUNT

I am here, speak!

UNKNOWN

You are very young.

MORDAUNT

People who wear my robe have no age.

UNKNOWN

Alas—speak softly—I have need of a friend in my last moments.

MORDAUNT

You are suffering a lot?

UNKNOWN

In the soul more than the body.

MORDAUNT

Speak, I am listening.

UNKNOWN

First, you must know who I am.

MORDAUNT

Speak.

UNKNOWN

I am—but I fear you will abandon me if you know who I am.

MORDAUNT

Have no fear.

UNKNOWN

I am the former executioner of Bethune.

MORDAUNT

The former executioner?

UNKNOWN

Oh—but for the last ten years I haven't worked—having a horror of myself—for the last ten years I quit my job.

MORDAUNT

You are horrified of your work?

UNKNOWN

For the last ten years, yes.

MORDAUNT

And before that?

UNKNOWN

Before that, I struck only in the name of law and justice. My condition let me sleep peacefully, sheltered as I was under justice and the law—but after this terrible night where I served as the instrument of a private vengeance—when I lifted with hate the sword on a creature of God—since that night—

MORDAUNT

What did he say there?

UNKNOWN

I have tried to stifle this remorse by ten years of good works—I have stripped the natural fury from those who shed blood, on every occasion I have exposed my life to save those who were in peril, and I have preserved alive humans, in exchange for those I have killed. That is not all. The wealth acquired in the exercise of my profession I have distributed to the poor. I come assiduously to churches, people who fled me are used to seeing me—some even love me—but it seems to me that God hasn't pardoned me—for the memory of this murder pursues me without ceasing.

MORDAUNT

You have committed a murder?

UNKNOWN

So it seems to me. Each night to see the ghost of that woman rise up.

MORDAUNT

It was a woman?

UNKNOWN

Oh—it was a cursed night.

MORDAUNT

What night was it?

UNKNOWN

The night of October 22, 1636.

MORDAUNT

(aside)

The same date he mentioned to Lord de Winter—Ah! Justice of Heaven! If I can learn all—

(he passes his hand over his face)

And who was this woman you assassinated?

UNKNOWN

Assassinated! And you too, you speak like the voice that has run in my head—assassinated— Did I assassinate rather than execute her? Am I a murderer and not an officer of justice?

MORDAUNT

Continue, continue! I know nothing and I can say nothing. When you have finished your story, we shall see. And now, how was it done? Speak! Tell all! Omit nothing!

UNKNOWN

(turning on his pillow)

It was evening. I lived in a house in a remote street. A man who had the air of being a great lord, although he wore the simple uniform of a Musketeer—knocked on my door and showed me an order signed "Richelieu". This order commanded obedience to the one who bore it.

MORDAUNT

The Order was indeed signed "Richelieu"?

UNKNOWN

Yes, but I dare say it was intended to serve another end than the one to which it was put.

MORDAUNT

Continue!

UNKNOWN

I followed this man, reserving the right to resist the order if it was suspect. At the town gate four other cavaliers waited for us. We traveled five or six leagues, somberly, gloomily, silently without exchanging a word. A hundred feet from Armentiers a man hidden in a ditch rose up "Here it is" said he—pointing by hand to a small isolated house—at the window of which shone a light. We cut across country and directed ourselves toward the house— There, other lackeys were stationed on the road. Each of them rose in his turn and joined us. The last, guarded the door. "Is she still there?" asked the man who brought me— "Still," he replied.

MORDAUNT

What am I going to hear, My God?

UNKNOWN

Then we dismounted and left the horses to the lackeys. He tapped me on the shoulder—the same one always—and he showed me through the window pane by the light of a lamp, a woman resting her elbows on a table, and said to me "Here's the one that must be executed."

MORDAUNT

And you obeyed?

UNKNOWN

I was going to refuse when suddenly—in looking at her more attentively, I recognized the woman in my turn.

MORDAUNT

You recognized her?

UNKNOWN

Yes—as a young woman she had seduced and ruined my brother. One night both had vanished with sacred vessels from a church. I found my brother on a gibbet. As for her, I had not seen her again.

MORDAUNT

Continue!

UNKNOWN

Oh, I knew well I ought to pardon her— It's the law of the evangelist—It's the law of God. The man in me stifled the Christian, it seemed that my brother's voice cried out for vengeance in my ear and I said, "It's all right, I will obey."

MORDAUNT

Continue!

UNKNOWN

Then the same one, always the same one, broke the window with a blow of his fist, the three others by the door. In seeing them she understood that she was lost—she yelled out—then pale and mute, as if in that one cry she had exhausted all her strength. She recoiled staggering until she was against the wall.

MORDAUNT

This is horrible!

UNKNOWN

Horrible, isn't it? But wait! Wait! Then they set up as accusers and each passed before her in his turn and reproached her. This one the assassination of his spouse, that one the poisoning of his mistress, and the other—The other was me—The other the dishonor and the death of his brother—There with a single voice, the same voice, a unanimous voice they pronounced the penalty of death, and I—

MORDAUNT

And you?

UNKNOWN

And I who had condemned her with the others—I, I—I undertook to execute her.

MORDAUNT

(rising)

Wretch! And you committed this crime?

UNKNOWN

On my salvation, I believed it to be justice.

MORDAUNT

And neither prayers nor tears for without doubt she prayed and cried—neither beauty nor youth for she was young and beautiful wasn't she? Nothing touched you?

UNKNOWN

Nothing! I believed she was the demon himself who had taken the form of that woman.

MORDAUNT

Ah—no more doubt now.

(He rises and goes to push the bolt in the door.)

UNKNOWN

You are leaving me? You abandon me?

MORDAUNT

No, no, be easy—I'm right here—Now let us see—reply—but without hiding anything, without being silent. Think that the frankness of your admissions alone can bring on you the mercy of Heaven. These five men, these five wretches, these five assassins. Who were they?

UNKNOWN

I didn't know their names, I have never known. They wore the uniforms of musketeers. That's all I know.

MORDAUNT

All?

UNKNOWN

No—one alone was dressed as a gentlemen—but he wasn't French—he was....

MORDAUNT

He was?

UNKNOWN

He was an Englishman.

MORDAUNT

His name.

UNKNOWN

I have forgotten his name!

MORDAUNT

You lie.

UNKNOWN

My God!

MORDAUNT

His name?

UNKNOWN

No, I cannot.

MORDAUNT

I am going to tell you his name—His name is Lord de Winter.

UNKNOWN

What do you say?

MORDAUNT

I said his name's Lord de Winter and that he was just here—I say that it was with him you left.

UNKNOWN

How do you know that?

MORDAUNT

Now—the name of this woman?

UNKNOWN

I never knew it. They called her "Milady" that's all.

MORDAUNT

"Milady"! But since she had seduced your brother, since she was the cause of the death of your brother—as you pretend—since this young woman escaped with sacred vessels from a church you ought to know the name of that young....

UNKNOWN

Yes, that one—I know it.

MORDAUNT

Her name?

UNKNOWN

It seems to me I am going to die.

MORDAUNT

Oh—don't die without having told me her name.

UNKNOWN

We'll you pardon me?

MORDAUNT

Her name, I tell you, her name!

UNKNOWN

Anne De Breuil.

MORDAUNT

(aside)

Ah—my presentiments didn't deceive me!

UNKNOWN

Now, now, that you know her name—pardon me, I am dying.

MORDAUNT

Me, pardon you? Pardon you. You know who I am?

UNKNOWN

Who are you then?

MORDAUNT

I am John Francis de Winter.

UNKNOWN

De Winter!

MORDAUNT

And this woman.

UNKNOWN

(rising)

This woman?

MORDAUNT

Well, this woman was my mother.

UNKNOWN

Your mother?

MORDAUNT

Yes, my mother, do you understand? My mother! Dead—without my knowing either where or how.

UNKNOWN

Oh—pardon me—! Pardon me!

MORDAUNT

Pardon you—? Pardon you? God perhaps—I never will.

UNKNOWN

From pity.

MORDAUNT

No pity for he who had no pity. Die cursed, die desperate—die and be damned.

(he strikes him with his poignard)

UNKNOWN

Help! Help!

VOICE

(outside)

Open! Open.

MORDAUNT

One Moment.

(he throws himself towards the window and jumps outside—the Innkeeper and his wife and Grimaud enter the chamber precipitously)

GRIMAUD

What's wrong with him?

UNKNOWN

Help!

INNKEEPER

The Monk—where is the monk?

UNKNOWN

He knifed me—and it was justice—the monk was her son.

GRIMAUD

What son?

UNKNOWN

(seeing Grimaud)

My God!

GRIMAUD

What?

UNKNOWN

You were one of the four lackeys of the four Lords that night.

GRIMAUD

Yes—

UNKNOWN

Well, this monk is her son.

GRIMAUD

The son of Milady?

UNKNOWN

Take this dagger—carry it to the four gentlemen and tell them what you know.

(he dies)

GRIMAUD

Ah. You are right—not a moment to lose. The Comte de la Fère, The Comte de la Fère.

INNKEEPER

(stopping him)

Well—and this man?

GRIMAUD

This man is dead.

CURTAIN

ACT I

Scene 1

D'Artagnan's chamber at the Hôtel de la Chevrette, of Mme. Turquenne, rue Tiquetonne, in Paris. At the right a door opening on a staircase, to the left center is an armoire closed by a curtain. Center, a large window.

MADELEINE

(alone)

(she holds a jerkin and brushes it)

Ah, here's a jerkin of blue velour that I didn't know Mr. D'Artagnan had. Without doubt it is with this that he makes his conquests, the ingrate. But what do I feel in his pockets? Some papers. Some will say that it's curiosity on my part, but after all, I have the right to be curious. Here's a love letter. I was sure of it.

(she unfolds a paper and reads it)

"Young turkey in mincemeat, stuffed carp, fried *à la* Mazarin, three bottles of wine from Anjou." This is already an infidelity. For the table of the Chevrette ought to suffice for a gallant man. But this infidelity I will still let pass.

(pulling out another letter)

(she reads)

"Sir, your adversary begins to enter convalescence. He has only three sword cuts which worry me, the others are healing into scars already." Ah! It's that Swiss sergeant who was installed in my hôtel much against my will—I can testify to that—and whom. D'Artagnan found established in his chambers on his return from the Flanders campaign. He left after five sword blows—poor dear man—

(folding a uniform)

Ah, D'Artagnan, you were amorous in those days. For you were jealous of the whole world especially the Swiss. Let's let that go.

This is the sacred doublet, the famous cassock of the musketeers, which we protect like a relic. Let's see if there isn't some relic in the pockets. Ah, ah papers tied with a favor. Ah traitor—a blue favor. Let's begin with this little tightly folded letter; this incontestably ought to be from a woman, "My dear D'Artagnan"— Her dear D'Artagnan" I confess that your memory pursued me even to my convent of Noisy Le See" Ah there's a letter, I hope—It is frightful!

(hearing noise outside)

Ah, my God—some uproar! It's him. Quickly, the uniforms, the doublets in this armoire—Well—Where did the Cassock go now— Ah here it is! When he leaves I will put the letter back—but this time although I've found the little cache I intend to know what it means.

(Enter D'Artagnan.)

D'ARTAGNAN

Ah, ah! Dear, Madame Turquenne, you're here.

MADELEINE

Yes Monsieur D'Artagnan, yes, you see I am straightening up.

D'ARTAGNAN

How useless it is to say "I am straightening up" The fact is, Madeleine....

(looking around him)

That you straighten up—often!

MADELEINE

Well it's the duty of a good wife, and I am yours.

(D'Artagnan looks at her sideways)

Your housekeeper, I mean— Oh! I have no pretension to aspire to the hand of a lieutenant of the Musketeers.

D'ARTAGNAN

Fine, Madame—I thought that your ideas of marriage carried off your wits.

MADELEINE

Alas, Monsieur D'Artagnan since you had such a categorical explanation with me!—

D'ARTAGNAN

My dear Madame Turquenne—short reckonings make long, long friends, besides I am not sure that the late Monsieur Turquenne is dead. I've seen husbands return just to hang their successor— But this is no time to debate the existence or non-existence of your first spouse, my dear Madeleine—it's time to find—

MADELEINE

What?

D'ARTAGNAN

Some ideas, many ideas, excellent ideas.

MADELEINE

Oh when you need them, *you* know where to find them.

D'ARTAGNAN

From you, right, my dear Madame Turquenne?

MADELEINE

No—but behind my firewood—for safekeeping.

D'ARTAGNAN

That's an old proverb of Athos'. There are more ideas in bottom of a simple bottle then in the head of forty academicians.

MADELEINE

You need many ideas?

D'ARTAGNAN

I need two—but of superior quality, you understand Madeleine? A bold, boiling energetic red seal. The other gay ingenious, fantastic green seal.

MADELEINE

Yes, with a slice of venison pie?

D'ARTAGNAN

That I've seen deeply in passing. It's extraordinary, my dear Madeleine Turquenne, how you read my heart.

(he folds her in his arms)

MADELEINE

(touching the pocket of his uniform) Wait? What have you here?

Some money?

D'ARTAGNAN

Indeed!

MADELEINE

You who always complain of lacking it?

D'ARTAGNAN

It's not mine. It's a deposit given me by the government.

MADELEINE

Oh! Deceiver that you are! I am sure that if I opened this secretary here—

D'ARTAGNAN

Madeleine, don't commit such an imprudence. It's a secretary to a secret which comes from a family and which has already slain three imprudent woman who had the boldness— But dear Madame Turquenne, you have spoken to me of fagots, I believe—one mustn't mention this in conversation.

MADELEINE

Ah, you can boast of having a manner of making women do what you wish.

D'ARTAGNAN

It's the result of fifteen years of study Madame Turquenne, that's the great advantage men have over woman—it's that wine, the more one tastes it, the better one knows it, while with woman—to the contrary.

MADELEINE

That's good, that's good—I'll go get you two bottles.

D'ARTAGNAN

Go, then, and shut the door.

(Exit Madeleine)

D'ARTAGNAN

(alone)

Huh! how this is set up. She has only one fault and that's never having enough of her own pockets. How she felt suddenly in mine the money of his Eminence. But—fool hardy! The money of Mazarin. Leprous green Italian pedant! Go! Hundred pistoles! I believed at first it was doubloons from Spain— That would have been worth the trouble—A hundred pistoles! "On account, Monsieur D'Artagnan"

Cursed Mazarin. "Yes, my lieutenant, begin by breaking legs and arms—exchange great blows of the sword, get a hole in your doublet with a pistol shot—and I will give you 100 pistoles—on account." And when is the accounting, contemptible wretch that you are! When I ask you for it, what? The least of things—a commission as Baron for Porthos who is dying to have a title? He takes a parchment—he writes names—he engraves the title and returns it to me without signing it. "But, the signature"— "On your return, Monsieur D'Artagnan"— "And if we don't return?" "Damnation, that's your concern. You'd better return." "And the Queen with her big nose—her Austrian lip and her beautiful insolent hands" "Monsieur D'Artagnan—Will be very devoted to Her Majesty." I will be devoted for a hundred pistoles to the King—and yet—yet—what am I saying—for the hundred pistoles or really twenty-five for Athos, twenty-five for Porthos, and twenty-five for Aramis.

(he laughs with pity)

It is true that if I don't find them—yes, but I must find them—they're worthy friends I have not seen for so many years. What a strange thing! One lives three, four, five years together, it seems we cannot live apart—they say it, they repeat it, they believe it—then comes a whirlwind which sends one to the south, the other to the north—another to the east, another to the west. One loses sight of each other and all is finished hardly even a letter. Now, let's not accuse each other; I received one from Athos—it was in 1643, six months or thereabouts after the death of Cardinal Richelieu—let's see, where was that? It…it was at the siege of Besancon, I recall. I was cut off. What did he say to me then? Ah, that he was living on a small estate. Yes, but where? I was reading it when a blast of wind carried Athos' letter to the other side of town. I let the wind take the letter to the Spanish who didn't need it and who ought to send it back to me today when I need it— Then let's think no more of Athos but of Porthos and Aramis. They too, wrote to me— Where are their letters? Ah, probably in my best cassock.

(he opens the Armoire)

Ah—Madeleine Straightened up. I'm very glad to know in what manner she straightens up—I will make her my compliment— Poor cassock! Here's one that's seen many adventures, and assisted at many battles—Also, it's kept its scars—here's the gap from a Biscayen who scorched my skin at the Bastion of Saint Gervais when our combat of heroic memory four against a hundred—twenty-five to one—just like his Eminence's pistoles. Here's a glorious scar—By whose hand was it made? I don't recall— It's singular that of all the most solid tissues which can be sewn up again—the most easy is the human skin. This buff cassock is not good for anything—and Monsieur D'Artagnan still values it. But for all that, I haven't found my letters—Is it the devil, then? Those unfortunate hundred pistoles have bewitched me; they were in this pocket here—the letters Ah! I believe, Madeleine who straightens up so well—Madeleine. Madeleine!

(Madeleine enters.)

MADELEINE

Here I am, here I am—I was going to the cellar.

D'ARTAGNAN

Fine—tell me, Madeleine—

MADELEINE

(aside)

He's been in the suitcase.

(aloud)

Red label.

(aside)

He must have discovered something.

(aloud)

Green style label, look!

D'ARTAGNAN

Dear Madame Turquenne—you overwhelm me—But put the bottles on the table and come here.

MADELEINE

Oh—what's that bag?

D'ARTAGNAN

Always government money—don't touch it—it burns your fingers—
Besides—we've got to talk.

MADELEINE

Well—let's talk.

D'ARTAGNAN

Madeleine, my child—we have been straightening up in the chamber of this good Monsieur D'Artagnan.

MADELEINE

So here we are!

(aloud)

But, yes—as usual—I cannot say no—you found me busy at it—

D'ARTAGNAN

To pick up—that is to say, in straightening up—we turned the pockets out—

MADELEINE

Me—No, no, never—!

D'ARTAGNAN

Madeleine, dear friend among the qualities which make you precious in my eyes, there is one which I wish you would find a way to
get rid of. You are horribly jealous and you know, Madeleine, a
great prophet said, or if he didn't say it, should have said, "Jealousy
causes women to go into drawers, tables and pockets of breeches"
you understand, Madeleine?

MADELEINE

Oh, one doesn't make that kind of reproach to me.

D'ARTAGNAN

Never mind—the moral is never lost—listen then—my dear Madeleine—if, as you are always saying, you want the best for me—God's blood!—don't make me the most unhappy of men!

MADELEINE

I don't know what to say.

D'ARTAGNAN

They were in my pocket, Madeleine—in this pocket, here—three letters. Do you understand quite well? The pocket does not have a hole in it. They were wrapped in blue ribbon.

MADELEINE

Ah—I see— That was very gallant.

D'ARTAGNAN

My little Madeleine, you see that I am very calm, very charming and that I haven't been the least violent—let's do things politely—admit to me that in folding my old clothes, this packet of letters fell out—right? And you put it back—let's see—give it to me—damnation!

MADELEINE

You know, Mr. D'Artagnan, that I don't do my lodger's washing.

D'ARTAGNAN

By God! Madeleine. I am not angry—no, no, no—I don't wish to be the least angry—but if someone doesn't find the address for me of Athos, Porthos, and Aramis—especially Porthos, and Aramis—especially Porthos—I will strangle everyone in the entire hôtel.

MADELEINE

Don't shout so, Mr. D'Artagnan.

D'ARTAGNAN

The address of Porthos, God's blood—damnation—Zounds!

MADELEINE

People will think we are fighting! Wait—someone's coming.

D'ARTAGNAN

(listening)

Oh My God! That step—three hundred pounds of weight—

(they come slowly)

I was stupid enough to believe that Providence was helping me. I thought it was the step of Porthos—

(a knock)

If I didn't know my worthy friend was on his estate, I don't know where, I would say that was Porthos' fist.

MADELEINE

Eh! But he's going to break down my door, this gentleman.

PORTHOS

(outside)

Well—doesn't one open the door for his friend anymore?

D'ARTAGNAN

It's Porthos' voice. Here's a coincidence!

(opens the door, Porthos enters with Mousqueton)

Porthos—in flesh and blood! Ah, dear friend!

(he jumps on his neck)

PORTHOS

With my faithful Mousqueton—as you see—don't you recognize me?

D'ARTAGNAN

Indeed. But I thank chance.

PORTHOS

Chance?

D'ARTAGNAN

Yes.

PORTHOS

It isn't chance that brought me here but your letter.

D'ARTAGNAN

Huh? My letter?

PORTHOS

Without doubt.

(giving him the letter)

It is indeed to me "To Monsieur du Vallon de Bracieux de Pierrefonds."

D'ARTAGNAN

Ah—de Pierrefonds—that's it. That's the name of the château. I recall it now. Never mind. It's not I who wrote you.

PORTHOS

Huh?

(reading)

Find yourself on the 20th of October 1648 at the Hôtel de la

Chevrette, Madame Turquenne, at Paris—where your old friend D'Artagnan lives who will be entranced to see you." That's what it says.

D'ARTAGNAN

Yes—but it wasn't written by me—that's all I can tell you.

MADELEINE

This is a letter that fell from one of Monsieur's old clothes.

PORTHOS

It's possible!

(seeing Madeleine)

But I ask your pardon, Madam—I didn't have the honor of seeing you.

D'ARTAGNAN

My dear Porthos, I present to you Madame Madeleine Turquenne— the most careful hôtel keeper in France and Navarre. A woman who never lets the papers of her tenants lie about untidily—but speak no more of that. You are here, Porthos. That's the thing. Why you came is of little importance—it will clear itself up—My dear, Madame Turquenne—Monsieur Porthos is going to have dinner with me.

MADELEINE

Then two red labels and two green labels— Let's go get them.

D'ARTAGNAN

Go ahead.

(Madeleine goes out)

D'ARTAGNAN

And now, dear friend, while waiting for the reinforcements Madeleine is going to procure for us—let's speak a word about these two bottles.

PORTHOS

Yes, willingly.

D'ARTAGNAN

God's blood—how well you look, dear Porthos.

PORTHOS

Yes—my health is fine.

(sighs)

D'ARTAGNAN

And still strong?

PORTHOS

More than ever. Do you know that at my château I have a library?

D'ARTAGNAN

Bah! You must be rich, my dear Porthos, that you allow yourself such useless expenditures?

PORTHOS

It came as part of the château, which I bought completely furnished.

D'ARTAGNAN

Good—but what has this library in common with your strength?

PORTHOS

Listen—in the library, there is a book.

D'ARTAGNAN

What—only a single book in your library?

PORTHOS

Not at all—wait—Mousqueton—how many books are there in my

library?

MOUSQUETON

Six thousand, sir.

PORTHOS

There are six thousand books.

(he sighs again)

D'ARTAGNAN

Wonderful!

PORTHOS

Well, amongst those six thousand books, there was a very interesting treatise on the twelve labors of Hercules. The exploits of Theseus and the feats of Milon of Croton. Well—down there to distract me, I did all that Milon of Croton had done.

D'ARTAGNAN

You have slaughtered a bull with a single blow of your fist?

PORTHOS

Yes.

D'ARTAGNAN

You carried it on your shoulders 500 paces?

PORTHOS

Six hundred.

D'ARTAGNAN

And you ate it in one day.

PORTHOS

Almost—there's only one thing I have been unable to do.

D'ARTAGNAN

What?

PORTHOS

It is stated in the book that Milon encircled his face with a rope, and that by inflating his muscles, he broke the cord.

D'ARTAGNAN

Ah—it's because your strength is not in your head, Porthos.

PORTHOS

No, it is in my arms.

D'ARTAGNAN

Hang it! How happy you are, Porthos! Rich, well dressed, and good!

PORTHOS

Yes, I am happy.

(he sighs for the third time)

D'ARTAGNAN

Porthos, there's the third sigh that you've uttered.

PORTHOS

You think so?

D'ARTAGNAN

Wait, my friend—they reveal that something torments you.

PORTHOS

Really?

D'ARTAGNAN

Do you have problems in your family?

PORTHOS

I don't have any family.

D'ARTAGNAN

Are you having trouble living with Madame du Vallon?

PORTHOS

She died almost three years ago.

D'ARTAGNAN

Ah—she's dead?

PORTHOS

Yes—right, Mousqueton?

MOUSQUETON

Almost two years ago, yes, sir.

D'ARTAGNAN

But then, dear boy, why are you sighing?

PORTHOS

Listen, D'Artagnan—I'm in need of something.

D'ARTAGNAN

What the devil can you lack? You have châteaux, fields, lands—
woods, mountains, you are rich, you're a widower, you're strong as
Milon of Croton, and you don't have to worry about being eaten one
day by lions.

PORTHOS

It's true—I have all that, but I am ambitious.

D'ARTAGNAN

You, ambitious, Porthos?

PORTHOS

Yes—all the world has something except me. You are a chevalier, so is Aramis—Athos is a Count.

D'ARTAGNAN

And you want to be Baron?

PORTHOS

Ah.

D'ARTAGNAN

(drawing the commission)

Stretch out your arm, Porthos.

PORTHOS

To do what?

D'ARTAGNAN

To stretch—again—well?

PORTHOS

A commission with French seals.

D'ARTAGNAN

Read!

PORTHOS

"Royal ordnance which awards the title of Baron to M. de Vallon.

D'ARTAGNAN

Baron—it's written.

PORTHOS

Ah, yes, but it is not signed.

D'ARTAGNAN

One cannot have everything at the same time. First, the commission. You will receive the signature later.

PORTHOS

And what must one do to get this signature?

D'ARTAGNAN

Ah—damnation! Quit your château—get back in harness, run adventures—and, as before—leave some of our skin on the way.

PORTHOS

The Devil! Then it's war you propose to me?

D'ARTAGNAN

Have you followed politics, dear friend?

PORTHOS

Me? To do what?

D'ARTAGNAN

Are you for the Prince or for Mazarin?

PORTHOS

Me? I'm for whoever makes me Baron.

D'ARTAGNAN

Good response, Porthos—and are you disposed to follow me?

PORTHOS

To the end of the world.

D'ARTAGNAN

Well, while waiting, go to your hôtel and put on your leather and armor.

PORTHOS

Ten minutes—ten minutes, that's all—I ask only ten minutes of you.

D'ARTAGNAN

Do you have a good horse?

PORTHOS

I have four—right, Mousqueton?

MOUSQUETON

Yes sir—Bayard, Roland, Joyeuse, and LaRochelle.

D'ARTAGNAN

In that case, don't lost time. Perhaps we'll leave today.

PORTHOS

Bah!

D'ARTAGNAN

I will come get you, my boy, when you are ready.

PORTHOS

As you will find us! Where are we going to?

D'ARTAGNAN

I don't know where.

PORTHOS

But if you don't know where we are going, we will undoubtedly get lost.

D'ARTAGNAN

Take it easy! Cardinal Mazarin will send us a guide.

PORTHOS

God! And when we return, I will be a Baron.

D'ARTAGNAN

That's agreed. Go equip yourself.

PORTHOS

Are you coming, Mousqueton?

MOUSQUETON

Yes, monsieur le Baron.

PORTHOS

(softening)

Ah! There's a word I will never forget in my life.

D'ARTAGNAN

(astonished—aside)

Mousqueton?

(Porthos leaves)

D'ARTAGNAN

(stopping Mousqueton)

Pardon me dear Mousqueton, but haven't you had the misfortune to lose a syllable of your name? How the devil did that accident happen to you?

MOUSQUETON

Sir—since from a lackey, I have been raised to the position of steward to monsignor—I have taken this last name which is more worthy—and which serves to make me respected by my subordinates.

D'ARTAGNAN

I understand. You and your master have each your ambition. He to lengthen his name, you to shorten yours. Go, Monsieur Mousqueton.

(Mousqueton leaves)

D'ARTAGNAN

(alone)

Decidedly it isn't as difficult as some people think to lead men. Study their interests, flatter their self love, goad them firmly, and shake hands. They will go where you wish. Look, here's Porthos engaged for the account of the Cardinal—it's always like that. Yes, but he isn't enough. We need Athos and Aramis—Oh! How they are going to need us these poor friends! It's true that Athos is a little old—he was always our elder—and then he drank horribly—he will be completely besotted. It's irritating that so noble a nature, such a powerful intellect, such a noble lord, a man who spends money like heaven makes hail, and who takes his sword in his hand with an air truly royal.... Well this noble gentleman, with proud eye,—this handsome cavalier, so brilliant under arms, that one is always astonished that he holds a simple sword and not a baton of command. Well—he will be transformed into some old twisted old man—red-nosed, eyes weeping—oh! What a frightful thing is wine....

(drinking)

...when it is bad.

(Enter Madeleine)

MADELEINE

M. le Comte de la Fère

D'ARTAGNAN

Who is this Comte de la Fère?

MADELEINE

Hell—I don't know—a handsome lord.

D'ARTAGNAN

Young.

MADELEINE

Thirty-five to forty.

D'ARTAGNAN

Bold manners?

MADELEINE

The air of a King.

ATHOS

(outside)

Well—dear D'Artagnan, are you visible?

D'ARTAGNAN

Ah! My God! That was his voice. Bring him in, Madeleine.

(Enter Athos)

D'ARTAGNAN

Athos, my friend.

ATHOS

D'Artagnan, my dear son, didn't you want to see me?

(they embrace)

D'ARTAGNAN

Oh, dear friend, yes—but the name de la Fère—which I never heard you use—

ATHOS

It's my ancestors' name which I've taken back. But if I've changed my name—I haven't changed my heart—or you either, right?

D'ARTAGNAN

Athos, I was thinking of you this very day. This very day I asked your address of Porthos.

ATHOS

Has he come too?

D'ARTAGNAN

Yes—do you know what must happen?

ATHOS

Continue, D'Artagnan—you say you asked my address from Porthos.

D'ARTAGNAN

Yes—I wanted to see you again.

ATHOS

In fact, poor friend, it's been a long while since we saw each other.

D'ARTAGNAN

Now I think of it, I have offered you nothing. Here's this little burgundy wine which you and Grimaud so rudely drank in the cellar of the hostler at Beauvais. Where is the Brave Grimaud? I hope he is still in your service.

ATHOS

Yes, my friend, but at the moment, he's traveling.

D'ARTAGNAN

Drink then.

ATHOS

Thanks D'Artagnan. I no longer drink—at least I drink nothing else than water.

D'ARTAGNAN

You, Athos, become a drinker of water? Impossible! You, the most intrepid drinker of all Monsieur Treville's musketeers.

ATHOS

Did you find I drank like everybody, my friend?

D'ARTAGNAN

No, it's true! You had at first a way of breaking the neck of a bottle which was all your own, and then you didn't drink like others. The eye of a drinker shines when he carries the cup to his mouth—your eye said nothing—but never was silence so eloquent. It seemed to murmur "Enter liquor and chase away cares."

ATHOS

In fact, that's the way it was, my friend.

D'ARTAGNAN

And the cause of these cares?

ATHOS

She doesn't exist any longer, my friend.

D'ARTAGNAN

So much the worse!

ATHOS

So much the worse?

D'ARTAGNAN

Yes, I'm going to propose a distraction to you.

ATHOS

What?

D'ARTAGNAN

It would be to take up our old life again. Let's see, Athos, if real advantages wait for you—wouldn't it be easy to start over in my company and that of our friend Porthos—the exploits of our youth?

ATHOS

So—you're making me a proposition?

D'ARTAGNAN

Neat and clear.

ATHOS

To enter a campaign?

D'ARTAGNAN

Yes.

ATHOS

On whose behalf—against whom?

D'ARTAGNAN

Ah! The Devil—you are pressing.

ATHOS

And very precise. Listen, D'Artagnan, there's only one cause in which a man like myself can be useful—it's that of the King.

D'ARTAGNAN

Exactly.

ATHOS

Yes, but listen—if by cause of the King, you mean to say that of Cardinal Mazarin—we will cease to listen to each other.

D'ARTAGNAN

The Devil. That's what tangles me up.

ATHOS

Let's not play to the end, D'Artagnan. Your hesitation and detours tell me enough on whose part you come—this cause—in effect—one cannot admit it aloud—and when one recruits for it, it is with lowered and embarrassed voice.

D'ARTAGNAN

Ah, my dear Athos.

ATHOS

Eh, my dear D'Artagnan. You know I don't speak of you for you are the pearl of brave men—loyal and bold. I speak of that Italian *miser* and intriguer, of this vulgar blob who strives to coiffeur his head with a crown which he has stolen from the queen—of this rogue who calls his role, the role of the King, and who counsels to put the princes of the blood in prison, not daring to kill them as would the Great Richelieu, of this skinflint who weighs his gold crowns—and who hides the parings from fear although he *cheats*; losing them the next day at play; of a clown now who mistreats the queen while counseling her reassuringly—and who is going in about six weeks to bring us to a civil war—to protect his pensions. If he's the master you propose to me—thanks so much!

D'ARTAGNAN

You are speaking out at your ease, my dear friend—you are happy, it appears in your golden mediocrity. Porthos has fifty or sixty thousand pounds rent perhaps. Aramis must have fifteen Duchesses who dispute over Aramis of Noisy le See as they fought over Aramis the Musketeer; he's still a sort of spoilt child. But me—am I in this world? I wore my buff and armor for more than twenty years—stuck in this insufficient grade, without advancing, without going back—without living. In a word, I am dead. Well, when it's a question for me to succeed a little, to go from lieutenant to captain. You will see me say "It's a rogue, a skinflint, a bad master." By God, dear friend, I know him as well as you— But find me a better or make me independently wealthy.

ATHOS

Well, that's what we thought, Aramis and I, my friend—and that's why I wrote to Porthos and Aramis to come here today.

D'ARTAGNAN

Ah—now I understand this coincidence.

ATHOS

You haven't seen them already?

D'ARTAGNAN

Porthos, yes—Aramis no.

ATHOS

It's strange! Aramis is the closest of the three. Aramis has only three or four leagues from his convent at Noissy le Sée to Paris.

D'ARTAGNAN

What do you expect, my dear! Aramis always has some penance to perform and with a vocation like his, one doesn't leave his convent so easily.

ATHOS

Well, you deceive yourself, my friend. Aramis has become a musketeer again and more musketeer than ever. He drinks, talks boisterously, compromises ladies—fights once a month and is called only the Cavalier d'Herbaly—still he is late—well, my friend, I suspect that he followed some skirt who made him lose the road to the rue Tiquetonne.

(Enter Aramis)

ARAMIS

Ah, my good friends, an adorable adventure—Bonjour, count, bonjour, dear D'Artagnan.

D'ARTAGNAN

Dear Aramis, here you are then.

ARAMIS

In person. Conceive a charming women I just met in church.

D'ARTAGNAN

And whom you followed.

ARAMIS

Right to her carriage.

D'ARTAGNAN

And from her carriage.

ARAMIS

Right to the door of a magnificent hôtel—an adorable person who reminded me of poor Marie Michon.

D'ARTAGNAN

Bad subject!

ATHOS

You see him! Always the same!

ARAMIS

Less hypocritical. For before, I admit it, my friends, I was a real hypocrite.

(Enter Porthos armed for war.)

PORTHOS

It's really true!

ARAMIS

Ah, it's you, Porthos! *Bonsoir*.

PORTHOS

But is it a surprise?

D'ARTAGNAN

Yes, my dear Porthos, a surprise arranged by Athos and most agreeable, as you see.

PORTHOS

(pressing Aramis to his breast)

Ah, dear Aramis, let me press you to my heart, dear friend.

ARAMIS

(choked)

Eh! say rather, it's not your heart that you're pressing me to, it's
your armor.

ATHOS

(giving his hand to Porthos)

Are you leaving for the crusades, my dear du Vallon?

PORTHOS

My word, I don't know—I only know I'm leaving—that's all.

D'ARTAGNAN

Hush! They are not with us.

PORTHOS

Bah!

ARAMIS

(low to Athos)

Have you spoken to them of the Prince and of the voyage that de Winter has made to Paris?

ATHOS

(low)

Useless, they are for Mazarin.

ARAMIS

(low)

We can act without them.

PORTHOS

(low to D'Artagnan)

What are we doing then?

D'ARTAGNAN

(low)

We will leave without them.

MADELEINE

(who all this while has put the cover on the table)

Gentlemen, the table is ready.

D'ARTAGNAN

Then let's profit from the wealth god sends us—it's true wisdom, is it not, Aramis? To table, Gentlemen, to table.

PORTHOS

That's much better reasoned, for I am dying of hunger.

ATHOS

(sitting)

And what is this napkin?

D'ARTAGNAN

Don't you recognize it, Athos?

ARAMIS

It's from the Fort of Saint Gervais.

PORTHOS

On which the other Cardinal had embroidered the Arms of France on the sides where it was pierced by three balls.

ATHOS

Why this napkin to me, friend?

D'ARTAGNAN

Because you were the greatest, the most noble, and the most brave of all, always!

ATHOS

Then gentlemen, by this flag, the only one which we ought to follow in the civil discords which are certainly going to sprout, and which will perhaps separate us, let us swear to each other to be good seconds in duels to be devoted friends in grave affairs—and joyous companions in pleasure.

D'ARTAGNAN

Oh—quite willingly.

ATHOS

And if ever fate makes us find ourselves in opposed camps—each time we meet in battle at the sole word "musketeer" let us put our sword in our left hand and hold each other with our right—right in the midst of carnage.

ARAMIS

Yes, by God, yes!

PORTHOS

Oh, that was well said, Athos, and how eloquent you always are—I have tears in my eyes—word of honor.

ATHOS

(with a somber air)

And cannot there be another pact between us besides one of friendship. Isn't there a pact of blood?

D'ARTAGNAN

You mean to say Milady?

ATHOS

And you—you think of her, D'Artagnan?

D'ARTAGNAN

Hold, Athos, you are terrible with your glance. Well, yes, gentlemen—I ask you, in thinking of that terrible night in Armentiers, of this man enveloped in a red cloak—who was the executioner, of this nocturnal execution, of this river which seemed to run in waves of blood—and of that voice which cried in the midst of the night "Let the justice of God take place." Haven't you sometimes felt moments of terror which resembled—?

ATHOS

Remorse? Right? I complete your thought. D'Artagnan have you experienced remorse? You?

D'ARTAGNAN

No—I have no remorse, because if we had let her live she would, without a doubt, have continued her work of destruction. But one thing which always astonished me, my friend—do you want me to say it?

ATHOS

Speak!

D'ARTAGNAN

It was that you—you the only one of us to whom that woman had done nothing—the only one who had no complaint against her—it was you, you Athos, so good, who prepared the expedition to Armentiers, who found the executioner, who conducted us to the cottage, and it was you who, as the envoy of divine justice pronounced sentence on her. And when I myself, my body shivering, my voice hesitating, my eyes in tears—when I was ready to pardon her—it was you who said: "Strike!"

ATHOS

This has always astonished you? Right?

D'ARTAGNAN

Yes, I admit it. If you hadn't spoken, I would have kept silent. But you were open with me from the first. Then I told you what I thought—Excuse me, Athos, if this can in some way wound you.

ATHOS

Friend, let me tell you an episode of my life that I have never told anyone. That will perhaps explain to you all—

ARAMIS

Speak, dear friend.

ATHOS

I do not recommend your discretion when you have heard what I am going to tell you—you will judge the thing terrible enough. I believe, if not to forget it, at least to bury it in the depths of your heart.

D'ARTAGNAN

We are listening to you, Athos.

ATHOS

Listen, I was twenty-five years old, I was a count—I was the first in my province over which my ancestors had reigned almost like Kings, I had a princely fortune—all the dreams of love—of happiness of glory which a twenty-five-year-old has. As to the rest—free entirely in my person, in my name—in my fortune. One day I met in one of my villages a young girl of sixteen years. Beautiful as love itself and as angels once were. Despite the naïveté of her age, in her burned an ardent spirit—she didn't please, she intoxicated. She lived with her brother, a young melancholy and somber man—both had come into the country in the past six months. They came from no one knew where, but seeing them, she so pretty, he so pious, no one thought to ask them where they came from. I was lord of the country. I could have seduced her or kidnapped her at my discretion. Unfortunately, I was an honest man and I married her.

D'ARTAGNAN

Then you loved her—?

ATHOS

Listen! I brought her to my château. I made her the first lady in the Duchy. Oh, one must be fair to her—she held her position perfectly.

D'ARTAGNAN

Well?

ATHOS

Well, one day we were hunting. Her horse frightened by the sight of a post, jumped. She fell unconscious. We were alone—I hurried to help her—and as she was suffocating in her clothes. I split them with my knife—guess what she had on her shoulder—D'Artagnan? A fleur de lys—she was branded!

D'ARTAGNAN

Horrible—what did you say to her, Athos?

ATHOS

The pure truth. My dear boy, the angel was a demon, the beautiful and naive young girl had stolen the sacred vessels from the church with her pretended brother, who was none other than her lover—I learned all this later. The brother having been taken and condemned.

D'ARTAGNAN

But she—what did you do with her?

ATHOS

Oh her—I was, as you have said—a great Lord, D'Artagnan, I had over my lands the right of judge—I finished loosening the clothes from the Countess—I took a rope and hanged her from a tree.

D'ARTAGNAN

A murder.

ATHOS

Not at all, unfortunately. For while I went off at a gallop from this fatal place and cursed country, someone without doubt came and saved her. She left France then, went to England where she married a lord and she had a child—then the Duke died and she returned to France, put herself in the service of Richelieu, cut the Queen's laces at a Ball, assassinated the Duke of Buckingham through Felton—and pardon me, dear D'Artagnan—to reopen this wound in your heart—poisoned the woman you adored, the charming Constance Bonacieux at the Augustine Convent.

D'ARTAGNAN

Thus, it was she?

ATHOS

Even so! All the evil that has been done to us came to us through her. Once she escaped me to commit these murders. This time, I swore she would not escape me again—and that she had run the course of her crimes. That's why I went to find the executioner of Bethune. That's why I brought you all to the cottage where she was hidden. That's why I pronounced the sentence—that's why, when you hesitated, Porthos, when you trembled Aramis, when you wept—D'Artagnan, that's why I said—"Strike".

D'ARTAGNAN

'Sblood, now I understand everything.

PORTHOS

And I, too.

ARAMIS

Bah! She was only an infamous person. Let's think no more of her.

D'ARTAGNAN

Happily of this event there remains not a trace.

ATHOS

She had a son with this Lord de Winter, brother of the one we knew.

D'ARTAGNAN

I know that well—since at the moment of her death you cried, "She didn't even think of her son."

ARAMIS

Eh! Who knows what has become of him? Kill the serpent, kill the brood. Do you think that de Winter, our companion—who led us to the accomplishment of this act of justice—would be amused to greet her son? Besides, if her son exists, he was in England, and hardly knew his mother. Then all was done in silence, in the night each of us has an interest in protecting the secret. This son knows nothing and can know nothing.

(They sit down.)

PORTHOS

Bah! The child is dead or the devil take me, or he might stir up trouble in this cursed England—let's eat.

MADELEINE

(entering)

The envoy of his Eminence.

ATHOS

What's wrong?

D'ARTAGNAN

Nothing!

ARAMIS

If it is a woman, dear friend, we will leave you.

D'ARTAGNAN

Not at all, gentlemen, it's a man.

PORTHOS

Well—if it's a man let him enter and come to dinner.

D'ARTAGNAN

No! He would doubtless be bad company for Athos and for Aramis. He's an envoy from the Cardinal—some wretch like himself; he has only a word to say to me. Stay there—and don't be upset if we speak low.

PORTHOS

Doubtless—but get rid of him promptly, the devil! It is true we were eating.

The three friends move to a corner.

(Enter Mordaunt dressed as a Puritan. Madeleine alone can see and hear him.)

MORDAUNT

Monsieur le Chevalier D'Artagnan.

D'ARTAGNAN

That's me, sir.

MORDAUNT

Lieutenant to the musketeers of His Majesty—company of M. de Traville?

D'ARTAGNAN

That's me.

MADELEINE

Aren't you expecting something, sir?

D'ARTAGNAN

Yes—a message from His Eminence—which must be sent to me by a trusted man.

MORDAUNT

(giving him a letter)

Here is the message, sir. It is I who am the messenger.

D'ARTAGNAN

(reading)

"Do what the bearer tells you and as for the dispatch which he brings you. Don't open it until you are out to sea."

MADELEINE

(aside)

Damn! Out to sea! Here I am a widow again.

MORDAUNT

You have read it?

D'ARTAGNAN

Yes.

MORDAUNT

You are ready to obey the orders His Eminence transmits to you by my voice?

D'ARTAGNAN

Without doubt— Am I not in his service?

MORDAUNT

Then equip yourself for war—and be with the friends you have promised the Cardinal to attach to his service next Tuesday at eight o'clock in the evening in the Dyke at Boulogne.

MADELEINE

(aside)

At the Dyke at Boulogne—it seems it is to England that they're going.

D'ARTAGNAN

Tuesday, you say, sir? And today is Saturday. Five days. Marvelous, I'll be there.

MORDAUNT

On Tuesday, eight o'clock in the evening at Boulogne, and remember, if you are not there at the day and time mentioned, I don't have the authority to wait for you a minute longer.

D'ARTAGNAN

It's needless to recommend timeliness to a soldier.

MORDAUNT

Good day, sir.

D'ARTAGNAN

Till we meet again.

(Mordaunt leaves making a slight bow to the three friends.)

MADELEINE

To us, too, now.

D'ARTAGNAN

You were listening to us?

MADELEINE

Me? Oh for heaven's sake—it appears that you are going to leave France?

D'ARTAGNAN

It's probable, Madame Turquenne.

MADELEINE

And that you are going to England?

D'ARTAGNAN

It's possible, dear friend.

MADELEINE

Well, I am going to profit from that to give you a recommendation.

D'ARTAGNAN

A recommendation.

MADELEINE

Yes, my sister runs the hostel "Home of the Stags" on the square of the Parliament—if you go there—

D'ARTAGNAN

She'll have my business.

MADELEINE

It's agreed.

D'ARTAGNAN

Certainly.

MADELEINE

Thanks.

(She leaves.)

PORTHOS

Now we can eat—

ATHOS

Didn't I tell you that Mazarin was a villainous man?

D'ARTAGNAN

Well—

ATHOS

Even his envoys are villainous men. What! Three gentlemen in the corner and he gave us a bow that hardly sufficed for one.

D'ARTAGNAN

Gentlemen, you must pardon him. I believe he's a Puritan.

ATHOS

He's come from England?

D'ARTAGNAN

I suspect so.

ATHOS

Then he might be an envoy from Cromwell?

D'ARTAGNAN

Perhaps.

ATHOS

In that case, he'll never see me again, your envoy.

PORTHOS

Nor me.

ARAMIS

Nor me.

ATHOS

And what's his name, this gentleman?

D'ARTAGNAN

I don't know.

PORTHOS

Gentlemen, let's eat.

GRIMAUD

(outside)

Number fifteen—door on the left?

MADELEINE

Yes.

GRIMAUD

(outside)

Fine!

D'ARTAGNAN

No. 15, the door on the left—that's here.

ATHOS

It's Grimaud's voice.

D'ARTAGNAN

Does he speak now?

ARAMIS

Oh, yes, on great occasions.

(Grimaud enters hurriedly.)

ATHOS

Oh! Gentlemen—something has happened. Grimaud—why this pallor—why this agitation?

GRIMAUD

Gentlemen—Milady de Winter had a child. The child is grown to a man. The tigress had a baby—the tiger is started—he's coming towards you—take care!

D'ARTAGNAN

What do you mean to say?

ATHOS

What are you saying?

GRIMAUD

I say, Monsieur Le Comte—that the son of Milady has left England—that he is in France, that he's coming to Paris, if he's not already here.

ARAMIS

The Devil, are you sure?

PORTHOS

Well—after all, when he comes to Paris, we have seen many others—there. Let him come!

D'ARTAGNAN

And besides, he's a child.

GRIMAUD

A child, gentlemen! You know what this child did? Disguised as a monk, he learned from the executioner of Bethune the complete story of his mother which he was unaware of—then after confessing him, for absolution, *he* planted a dagger in his heart—it's still red and wet!

ARAMIS

Have you seen him?

GRIMAUD

Yes.

D'ARTAGNAN

Do you know his name?

GRIMAUD

I don't know it.

ATHOS

(rising)

I know it. His name is the Avenger.

CURTAIN

ACT I

Scene 2

A salon at de Winter's in the place Royale.

DE WINTER

You were saying, Count.

ATHOS

I say that Grimaud arrived as he expired, that he brought us the still smoking dagger.

DE WINTER

Then he knows everything.

ATHOS

Everything except our names.

DE WINTER

But how? Why did he leave England?

ATHOS

He was still in England?

DE WINTER

Eh, yes.

ATHOS

What was he doing there?

DE WINTER

He was one of the most ardent followers of Oliver Cromwell.

ATHOS

Why did he rally to that cause? His father and his mother were Catholic, I believe.

DE WINTER

The King, on my request, declared him a bastard, despoiled him of his rights and forbade him to use the name de Winter—his hate for Charles I has pushed him to Cromwell.

ATHOS

And what's he call himself now?

DE WINTER

Mordaunt.

ATHOS

Fine, I'll remember it. Providence has warned us, we will be on our guard. But, let's return to the affair which brought you to Paris, my Lord.

DE WINTER

Two words first. You still have as friends Messieurs Porthos and Aramis?

ATHOS

And D'Artagnan, milord. We are still as before, four friends devoted to each other. Only, when it's a question of being partisans we are only two: Aramis and me.

DE WINTER

I recognize you well in that. You have adopted the side of the Princes—the great cause—it was the only one agreeable with your noble and generous character. I won't hide from you that I came to France in this hope.

ATHOS

Are we then of some concern in your voyage?

DE WINTER

Yes, Count, I have need of you both—you have forewarned Monsieur Aramis?

ATHOS

Wait, he's here.

(Enter Aramis.)

DE WINTER

Good day, Chevalier—you came just at the right time. I was going to ask the Count's permission to present you both to the Queen of England.

ATHOS

To the Queen of England?

DE WINTER

To Madame Henriette de France.

ATHOS

Pardon, milord, I don't know Her Majesty except from her misfortunes there and her exile here.

DE WINTER

But I know you and I have promised her this very morning to bring you to her.

ATHOS

At this house?

DE WINTER

No, at the Carmelites—are you ready gentlemen?

ATHOS

At your orders, milord.

(Enter Tomy.)

DE WINTER

What do you want, Tomy?

TOMY

Her Majesty's Valet de chambre asks to deliver a letter from his august mistress to your Lordship.

DE WINTER

Enter, Parry, enter—what news from Her Majesty?

(Enter Parry.)

PARRY

Sound of body, but very sad of heart, milord.

DE WINTER

You are charged with something for me?

PARRY

This letter, milord.

DE WINTER

(breaks the seal—opens the letter and reads)

"Milord, I fear, if you come to find me at the Louvre or the Carmelites, you will be followed or that we will be overheard. I think it better to come to you. Since the step I am taking is against royal custom, the less likely we will be spied on. Wait for me there rather than coming to me. I will be there almost as soon as my messenger— Yours affectionately, Henriette." Fine, Parry, I will wait for your mistress.

TOMY

Milord permits me a single word?

DE WINTER

Speak.

TOMY

I've questioned Mr. Parry—and this man who—this morning followed him here.

DE WINTER

Well?

TOMY

He is still at the corner of the street. Mr. Parry saw him and recognized him at the signal I gave him.

DE WINTER

And you know who this man is perhaps?

TOMY

He's turned from my sight.

DE WINTER

Well, I will be careful—go—thanks, Parry!

(Exit Parry.)

ATHOS

This letter upsets your plans, milord?

DE WINTER

No, Count.

ATHOS

It seems to annoy you.

DE WINTER

She astonishes me, that's all—because of the great honor she is do-ing me.

PARRY

(opening to door)

Milord.

DE WINTER

Is it the person who did me the honor of writing to me?

PARRY

Exactly—her coach is stopped at the door.

DE WINTER

Go receive her, Parry, go.

ARAMIS

A woman?

DE WINTER

No, a queen.

ATHOS

Her Majesty, Madame Henriette.

DE WINTER

Yes, gentlemen.

ATHOS

Then we will retire, milord.

DE WINTER

(raising a tapestry)

Not at all—on the contrary, stay here and listen to what is said between Her Majesty and me—you will be free to show yourselves or remain hidden—if you show yourselves it means you accept. If you remain hidden, it means you refuse.

ARAMIS

But milord, we don't understand.

DE WINTER

You will understand later—go in—go in.

(They step behind the tapestry which de Winter lowers.)

(Enter the Queen dressed in black.)

DE WINTER

Open both doors, Tomy—

(Tomy opens and bows.)

QUEEN

(lifting her veil)

Ah—milord—it is really you! I feared I had misread. I feared that this letter bearing your name had deceived me—you come on the King's behalf, milord? Speak quickly—what have you to tell me?

DE WINTER

I have to give this message to Your Majesty.

(falling to his knees and presenting the queen with a gold box)

QUEEN

(opening the box and extracting a letter)

Milord, you have brought me things I haven't seen for a long time—gold, a letter, and a devoted friend.

DE WINTER

Your Majesty overwhelms me.

QUEEN

And now let's see what is in this precious letter—Ah it's in the handwriting and even bears the signature of my Charles.

(reading)

"Madam—and dear spouse—here everything is on the edge. All of my resources are concentrated in the camp at Newcastle, from which I've written you. I await the army of my rebel subjects with the aid of my brave Scotch. I am going to struggle one last time against them. If I win, I prolong the struggle. If I lose, I lose everything. In this latter case, I have only to reach the coast of France. But would you want to receive an unfortunate King bringing such a funereal example to a country already disturbed by civil discords? The bearer of these presents whom you know is one of my oldest and most faithful friends."

(she interrupts and offers her hand to the Lord de Winter)

Oh yes, milord.

(continuing)

"The bearer of these presents will tell you Madam what I cannot confide to the risks of an accident. He will explain to you what steps I expect of you and I charge him also with my blessing for my dear children who are in France and of all the sentiments of my heart for you, madam, my dear spouse. Charles—still King." God permit that our two children—the Princess Elizabeth and the Duke of Gloucester who are in London are well— Ah my God! Let him not be King, let him be vanquished, exiled, proscribed, but let him live! Let my children renounce the throne of their father—but let them live. Oh, tell me, milord is the position of the King indeed hopeless?

DE WINTER

More hopeless than he himself believes, Madam.

QUEEN

And what does he expect of me in this extremity? Let's see—speak quickly.

DE WINTER

That Your Majesty ask help from Mazarin—or at least a refuge in France.

QUEEN

Alas, Milord, do you think that I waited for this letter to do what I could over here?

DE WINTER

Well?

QUEEN

Well—aid—asylum—money—Mazarin has refused me everything.

DE WINTER

What! He has refused asylum to King Charles? The brother-in-law of King Louis XIII and the uncle of King Louis XIV?

QUEEN

Alas, I disturb and tire him very much. My presence and that of my daughter—a much stronger reason than that of the King—Milord, listen—it's sad and very shameful to tell, but we spent winter at the Louvre—Henriette and I—without money, without linen, almost without bread—staying often hidden in bed much of the day because there was no heat—so that we were almost dead—both of us from hunger and misery without the charity that the parliament wished to provides us.

DE WINTER

Horror! The daughter of Henry the IV dying of hunger in this country where her father saw to it that the least peasant had more than was necessary. Why, didn't you address yourself first to us, Madam? He had split his fortune with you madam—he had put all that he possessed at the foot of his queen.

QUEEN

You see, indeed, de Winter, that I can do only one thing—that's return to England with you.

DE WINTER

To do what, madam?

QUEEN

To die with the King since I cannot save him.

DE WINTER

Ah, madame, that is especially what the King fears—and he begs you, and if need be, orders you not to do that.

QUEEN

Milord—the King speaks from a heart that is kind, from a heart that loves. Is he unaware that the worst sorrow is uncertainty? One can get used to a misfortune one can see face to face. Once it is known, one can find resources to resist it. But a vague misfortune, distant, indefinite, untouchable, unknown—there's no other remedy but prayer. And I have prayed so much, milord without anything having changed in the King's fate or in mine that I begin to despair. Milord, if the King in the extremity which he finds himself wishes to distance himself from me—then it is because the King does not love me.

DE WINTER

Oh, madame, you know yourself that such an accusation is unjust. No, the King fears danger no more than hard work.

QUEEN

Dangers—hard work—am I not used to them? Didn't I alone, under the pretext of taking my daughter to Holland—solicit arms, money, and aid from William of Orange? On my return wasn't I caught in a terrible storm, as if, against our unfortunate cause, not only the wrath of men but of God was unleashed? In the midst of this tempest did I leave the bridge of the boat? To all the representations of the captain and the crew that I encouraged by my presence—did I reply to anything except by saying there was no example in history of a queen being drowned—then after having lost two vessels and one to whom I gave aid being pushed back to the shores of Holland—did I hesitate at the first favorable wind to put to sea again? This time, God willing—I was allowed to persevere. But, hardly landed, the house in which I was taking refuge was surrounded, attacked. You know it, my Lord because it was you who came to rescue me. Where did you find me milord? Speak! At the breach: the cannon had just made this house crumble—in the midst of fire, wounded, dead, all bloody with the blood of my defenders and my own—for a splinter of wood had wounded me. In seeing you, milord—did I think of myself? For when it became necessary for me to dress like a man to get to him, did I hesitate? Three days and three nights you saw me at your side. Did I sigh even once? Did I make a complaint? Did I ask for more for myself than the least of your officers? No, hard work, privations, dangers—all are forgotten when I saw my husband and king again. A full year I passed with him—in the mountains, in the camp, almost always under a tent, very rarely in a house. Or a palace—alas! It's been a long time since a palace was for us! Who forced me to leave him? Only the will of God and love for my child. I left to be a mother. I don't fear death, I was afraid of killing my poor Henriette. I spoke to you of misery milord. But at this moment am I not the most miserable of women? Here at least I have the Louvre destitute as it is, offered to me. What did I have at Exeter? A simple cottage! The Convent of the Carmelites even more somber. My poor child spends the day on a pallet, without a mattress or blanket. It was then I received a messenger from the Queen, my sister—this messenger brought me two hundred thousand pounds. Did I keep a pistole for myself? No, to the last shilling, I sent it all to Charles because he's everything to me—you see. Then when he made me leave him to return to France—oh! Milord! You were there! You saw my sorrow—my tears, my despair! And when you come to me to say that his position is yet more desperate, that he no longer believes in himself, that his liberty is menaced—his life per-haps! You speak to me of dangers and difficulties—to me whose reign has been a long difficulty and whose life has been a long dan-ger? Ah, milord! If the King tells you to say that, he lacks memory; and if you oppose what I say, you, milord—you lack pity!

DE WINTER

It is exactly because he recalls all you have suffered that the King wishes you to stay in France—it is exactly, pardon me the word be-cause I have pity for my queen, that I cannot wish her to go to Eng-land.

QUEEN

Well let's not speak of it anymore, milord. I don't wish to place you between the respect you owe your Queen and the obedience you owe your King. Speak of yourself—speak of him—have you no other end, in coming to France than what you have discussed with me?

DE WINTER

Indeed, Madam.

QUEEN

Well—speak—we'll see.

DE WINTER

Once in France, I knew four gentlemen.

QUEEN

(very sad)

Four gentlemen! And that's the aid that you count on to bring to a King on the point of losing his throne?

DE WINTER

Ah, if I had had only these four, I would answer for many things, Madam. Haven't you heard tell of four gentlemen who once sus-tained Anne of Austria against Cardinal Richelieu?

QUEEN

Yes, it's a tradition in the court.

DE WINTER

Of four gentlemen who crisscrossed France, despite all ambushes shedding their blood during the route they followed to go to England to find the famous string of diamonds which almost cost Anne of Austria her throne?

QUEEN

Yes.

DE WINTER

These four gentlemen, if I told you all they had done, Madame, you would think I was recounting a chapter from Ariosto or that I was reading you a Canto from Tasso. But alas, of these four valiant men, I learned this morning, there remain only two.

QUEEN

The two others are dead?

DE WINTER

Much worse than that! The two others are with Cardinal Mazarin!

QUEEN

And the two who remain?

DE WINTER

The two who remain, madame, I don't yet know if they are able to leave Paris or even if—being free, they wouldn't be frightened of the dangers which threaten such an enterprise, and if they will consent to follow me to England.

(Athos and Aramis come from behind the drapery.)

ATHOS

Milord, tell Her Majesty that for such a worthy cause, we would go to the very ends of the earth.

QUEEN

Oh! My God! These gentlemen overheard us.

DE WINTER

And you see, madam, that you can say anything before them.

QUEEN

Thanks, gentlemen. Thanks! Milord, the names of these brave gentlemen that I may hold them religiously in my memory.

DE WINTER

Monsieur le Comte de la Fère and Monsieur le Chevalier d'Herblay.

QUEEN

Gentlemen in the past I had surrounding me, counts, armies, treasuries. At a sign of my hand, all this was employed in my service. Today, look around me—to accomplish a design on which depends the health of a realm and the life of a King—I have only Lord de Winter, a friend of twenty years and you gentlemen—whom I have known only for twenty seconds.

ATHOS

It is enough, madame, if the lives of three men repurchase that of your Royal spouse. Now—tell us what we must do?

QUEEN

(to Aramis)

But you sir, have you like the Comte de la Fère, compassion for so much misfortune?

ARAMIS

I, madam, from custom, always go where the Count goes. I do it, without asking him where he's going—but when it's a question of serving Your Majesty, I am not with him, Madame, I precede him.

QUEEN

Well, gentlemen, then you intend to devote yourself to the service of a poor princess that the entire world has abandoned? That's what it's a question of doing. The King is alone in the midst of the Scotch whom he defies, although he is Scotch himself. I ask much, I ask too much, perhaps, although I have not the right to ask—but still if you agree to serve this great cause of royalty in the person of King Charles—be his friends, be his protectors, march to his side in prison, stand in front and behind him in his house—where ambushes press on him more perilous than all the risks of war. And in exchange for all this sacrifice you make for me, I promise you not to reward you, this word would injure you, I am sure of it.—Besides, it sits poorly for an exile who begs to speak of reward, but—to love you as a sister would love you—and to prefer you above all others except my children and my spouse.

ATHOS

Madam, when must we leave?

QUEEN

Then you agree? Ah, gentlemen, here is the first moment of hope I have known in the last five years. You understand it is not his throne, it is not his crown I commend to you it is the life of my Charles, of my spouse, of my King, that I am putting in your hands.

ATHOS

Madame, all that two men who never retreat from danger can do—expect it of us.

(The Queen gives her hand to the gentlemen who fall to their knees.)

QUEEN

Yet once more, oh! With all my soul, thanks, gentlemen.

DE WINTER

Does Your Majesty want me to accompany her back?

QUEEN

No—you might be recognized.

ATHOS

But we, madame, do not run the same risk.

QUEEN

I have my carriage, gentlemen.

ATHOS

(bowing)

Then we will follow humbly, and from a distance, Your Majesty's carriage.

QUEEN

Goodbye Count, tell the King that my days are nothing but long miseries and my nights long insomnia—that all my life is but an eternal prayer—but when God reunites us, be it on Earth or in heaven—all will be forgotten.

(She leaves, followed an instant later by Athos and Aramis.)

DE WINTER

(looking through the window)

Poor Queen.

(Mordaunt appears and stays on the sill of the door. De Winter leaves the window and perceives Mordaunt)

Who is there? What do you wish, sir?

MORDAUNT

Oh! Oh! Don't you by chance recognize me?

DE WINTER

Indeed, sir. And the proof is that I repeat to you in Paris what I told you in London—your persecution tires me—withdraw, sir, or I will call my servants.

MORDAUNT

Ah—my uncle!

DE WINTER

I am not your uncle. I don't know you.

MORDAUNT

Call your people, if you wish. You won't chase me out of Paris like you did out of London. As for denying that I am your nephew, think twice—now I have learned certain things of which I was unaware a year ago.

DE WINTER

Eh! And what does it matter to me what you have learned?

MORDAUNT

Oh—it matters a whole lot to you; I am sure of it, and you are going to be of my opinion soon. When I came to you the first time in London, it was to ask you what became of my inheritance. When I came to you the second time, it was to ask who had besmirched my name. And both times, I remember you drove me away. But this time, I came to ask you a question much more terrible than all those questions. I came to you, as God came to the first murderers—and said, "Cain what have you don't to your brother?" Milord, what have you done to your sister?

DE WINTER

To your mother?

MORDAUNT

Yes—to my mother, milord.

DE WINTER

Find her where she's gone, unfortunate one, and ask Hell—perhaps Hell will reply to you?

MORDAUNT

(advancing on de Winter).

I asked the Executioner of Bethune and the Executioner of Bethune told me— Ah! You understand me now. With this word all is explained, with this key, the abyss opens. My mother inherited from her husband, you assassinated my mother. My name assured me paternal wealth—you have taken my name from me—I am no longer astonished that you don't know me. It is unseemly to recall one's nephew when one is his despoiler—the man who impoverishes him—when one is a murderer—the man who made him an orphan.

DE WINTER

You wish to penetrate this horrible secret, sir? Well—so be it— know then who it was. This woman—of whom you today ask me for an accounting—this woman poisoned my brother—and to inherit from me she tried to assassinate me in my turn. What do you say to that?

MORDAUNT

I say that she was my mother.

DE WINTER

She stabbed the unfortunate Duke of Buckingham through means of a man otherwise just and good—what do you say to this crime of which I have proof?

MORDAUNT

She was my mother!

DE WINTER

Returned to France after the assassination, she poisoned a woman who loved one of her enemies in the convent at Bethune. This crime will persuade you of the justice of her chastisement. This crime I can prove.

MORDAUNT

She was my mother!

DE WINTER

Then, charged with murders, with debauchery odious to all, menacing still like a panther thirsty for blood, she fell under the blows of men she had made desperate, and who never caused her the least harm. She found, in default of natural judges, judges her hideous murders had evoked. And this executioner who told you everything, ought to tell you he thrilled with joy in avenging on her the suicide of his brother. Perverted daughter, adulterous spouse, unnatural sister, murderess, poisoner, execrable to all. To those who knew her, to all nations that had received her in their bosoms, she died cursed by heaven and earth. There you have this woman.

MORDAUNT

Silence sir! She was my mother! Her disorders I do not know. Her vices I do not know. Her crimes I do not know. She was my mother! So, I warn you, listen carefully to the words I am about to speak, and engrave them in your memory so that you will never forget them. This murder which has ravished me of everything, which was impoverished me, this murder which has corrupted me—infuriated me—made me implacable—I will ask an accounting from your accomplices when I learn who they are—of all my enemies in fact, without excepting even King Charles the First.

DE WINTER

Do you intend to assassinate me, sir? In that case, I truly recognize you as my nephew for you will truly be your mother's son.

MORDAUNT

No—I won't kill you, at this time at least—for without you, I cannot discover the others. But when I know the names of the four men from Armentiers, tremble sir, tremble for yourself and your accomplices! I have already stabbed without pity, without mercy one—and he was the least culpable of you all.

(He leaves.)

DE WINTER

My God—I thank you that he only knows me!

CURTAIN

ACT I

Scene 3

The Dyke at Boulogne—one sees at the right the house of a fisherman—in the rear. The Brig *The Parliament*. Also at anchor the Corvette *L'Éclair*. To the left a stairway which leads to a lighthouse.

MORDAUNT

(walking on the Dyke and with him is André, the captain of the Brig)

Well—Captain André?

ANDRÉ

No one yet, sir.

MORDAUNT

You have been to the hôtel "The English Arms"?

ANDRÉ

Yes, sir.

MORDAUNT

And you asked if two gentlemen named Monsieur D'Artagnan and Du Vallon had arrived from Paris?

ANDRÉ

No one has seen them yet.

MORDAUNT

Nor anyone who resembles them?

ANDRÉ

Three gentlemen arrived just as I was speaking to the hôtel manager. I had a moment of hope but I was deceived. They went to the lodge at the Sword of Henry IV yet one of the three came in. The two others threw the bridles of their horses into the hands of their lackeys and asked the way to the port.

MORDAUNT

Let them remember well that I gave them just until eight o'clock. I won't wait a minute more. At eight o'clock, exactly, Captain, you will sail.

ANDRÉ

Well, sir, I am at your orders.

(Enter Parry, approaching André.)

PARRY

Sir, aren't you the skipper of this ship?

ANDRÉ

Yes, sir.

PARRY

You are leaving this evening?

ANDRÉ

At eight o'clock.

PARRY

Can you give passage to me and my sister?

ANDRÉ

(low to Mordaunt)

You hear?

MORDAUNT

(low)

Make sure she is his sister.

ANDRÉ

(to Parry)

But do you know our destination?

PARRY

Yes, you go to Newcastle and as Newcastle is the frontier of Scotland, we will have only the Tyne to cross to be in our country.

ANDRÉ

(to Mordaunt)

What's to be done?

MORDAUNT

See the woman, try to learn who she is what she wants and if necessary, I will see her myself.

ANDRÉ

Where is your sister?

PARRY

(pointing)

In this house. Shall I call her?

ANDRÉ

No—don't disturb her. I am going to speak to her myself.

MORDAUNT

Go! Ah! Ah! I believe here are our men.

ANDRÉ

(looking)

No these are the two travelers who asked the way to the port at the hôtel Sword of Henry the IV.

MORDAUNT

They came by the Paris route?

ANDRÉ

Yes.

MORDAUNT

I will perhaps get some news out of them. Go then!—But you understand—promise nothing until I've seen her myself.

ANDRÉ

Oh! Be easy!

(to Parry)

Come, sir.

(Parry & André go out.)

MORDAUNT

(alone)

No—it's not them. But in truth, if I don't deceive myself, it's their two friends—the same who were with them in the Chambers of Monsieur D'Artagnan when I went there. We won't meet them at first.

(Mordaunt in the foreground—Athos and Aramis crossing on a sluice and stopping in the middle.)

ARAMIS

What do you think of this ship, Athos?

ATHOS

That it is sailing, too. But that it cannot be ours—this is a brig and ours is a corvette; this one is in harbor and ours is waiting at sea. This one is called *The Parliament* and ours, de Winter, told us, is called *L'Éclair*.

MORDAUNT

De Winter! Did they pronounce the name de Winter?

ARAMIS

Hush! There's a man who seems to hear us.

ATHOS

He's wasting his time—for we have said nothing, it seems to me—which cannot be heard.

ARAMIS

Never mind—speak of something else—for now—for that man is approaching us.

MORDAUNT

(waiting for Athos and Aramis to arrive)

Pardon, gentlemen, I am not deceived. I'm sure, I've had the honor of seeing you in Paris, I believe.

ATHOS

You, sir? I don't recall on my count having had that honor.

ARAMIS

Nor I, sir.

MORDAUNT

At M. D'Artagnan's, about four days ago.

ATHOS

Ah—it's true, sir. I recall perfectly. I pray you excuse this fault of memory.

ARAMIS

Very fine.

MORDAUNT

Could you tell me if M. D'Artagnan is still in Paris?

ATHOS

We left him three days ago at the Hôtel de la Chevrette.

MORDAUNT

And did he tell you nothing of preparing for a voyage?

ATHOS

No, sir.

MORDAUNT

Excuse me, gentlemen for disturbing you—and receive my thanks for your compliance.

(He bows and leaves.)

ARAMIS

What do you say of that questioner?

ATHOS

A boring provincial.

ARAMIS

Or a spy who informs.

ATHOS

It's possible.

ARAMIS

And you have replied to him thus?

ATHOS

Nothing would authorize me to reply otherwise, he was polite towards us, and I was polite to him.

ARAMIS

No matter, in our position—we must be wary of the whole world.

ATHOS

It's a little too soon for you to make this recommendation. You spoke the name "de Winter".

ARAMIS

Well?

ATHOS

Well—it was at that name the young man stopped.

ARAMIS

You noticed that?

ATHOS

Perfectly.

ARAMIS

Reason the more then, when he spoke to us to invite him to pass on his way.

ATHOS

A quarrel?

ARAMIS

And since when does a quarrel frighten you?

ATHOS

A quarrel always frightens me when I wait some role and that this quarrel could prevent me from playing it. Besides, do you want me to admit something to you?

ARAMIS

What?

ATHOS

I perfectly recognized this young man as the messenger of Mazarin.

ARAMIS

Ah, really!

ATHOS

But I wanted to see him close up.

ARAMIS

For what?

ATHOS

Aramis, you're going to mock me. You're going to say that I always repeat the same thing. You're going to take me for the most fearful of visionaries.

ARAMIS

Why?

ATHOS

To whom does this young man resemble—as much as a man can resemble a woman?

ARAMIS

Oh—by God! I believe you are right, Athos—that mouth fine and open, the nose cut like the beak of a bird of prey—the eyes that seem always at the order of the mind and never of the heart—If he was the monk!

ATHOS

In spite of me, I thought it.

ARAMIS

And you didn't destroy the serpent?

ATHOS

Are you mad? Without being sure? Besides, were we certain, this young man has done nothing to us.

ARAMIS

Ah, there's where I recognized my Athos—childish from greatness—imprudent from loyalty. Well, if I knew it was he, I would break his head against the first stone I can find.

ATHOS

Hush—de Winter.

ARAMIS

We were just speaking of him! He must know his nephew!

ATHOS

We would have the air of frightened children.

ARAMIS

It's true. Let us let things go—and defy the young man if we find him again—but is it really de Winter?

ATHOS

Yes, you see, there are our lackeys who follow him twenty paces in the rear—at the corner of the fort. I recognize Grimaud, by his big stiff head and his long legs and my little Blaisois by his provincial bearing. It's he who is carrying our carbines.

ARAMIS

It's true. But where is our friend? He resembles one of the damned in Dante whose necks Satan has dislocated and who look at their talons. What's he looking behind him for?

(Enter de Winter.)

(The night comes and the lighthouse is illuminated.)

DE WINTER

Ah, you here, Gentlemen! I am quite easy to have rejoined you—we are going to leave instantly, aren't we?

ARAMIS

We do not delay you, milord, although I don't care for the sea much by day and still less by night. But what have you there that puts you so out of breath?

DE WINTER

(looking behind him)

Nothing, nothing—still in passing behind the fortification it seemed to me—but let's leave. Hold—see down there the boat by the lighthouse. That's our Corvette—which is at anchor—I wish we were already embarked.

ARAMIS

Ah, That! You forgot something, milord?

DE WINTER

No, it's a preoccupation.

ATHOS

(to Aramis)

He's seen him.

DE WINTER

Let's go down, gentlemen—Hola! Captain!

(A man hidden in a boat rises)

You are the boatman who must conduct us to the Corvette—
L'Éclair, right?

BOATMAN

Yes, sir.

DE WINTER

Help our lackeys then.

BOATMAN

Come this way.

(Mordaunt reappears on the other side of the jetty and mounts the stair leading to the lighthouse. The three gentlemen embark.)

ARAMIS

(to Athos)

Oh! Oh! There's our young man again—does he intend to stop our embarking?

ATHOS

Why do you think he has that intention? He is alone and we are seven if you count the boatman.

ARAMIS

Never mind—assuredly he has it in for us—

DE WINTER

Who's that?

ARAMIS

The young man.

DE WINTER

What young man?

ARAMIS

Wait—the one who is down there—at the lighthouse.

DE WINTER

It's him. I thought I recognized him.

ATHOS

Who is he?

DE WINTER

The son of Milady.

GRIMAUD

The Monk.

MORDAUNT

Yes, it's me, my uncle! Me, the son of milady! Me the monk! Me the secretary and friend of Cromwell—and I recognize you and your companions.

ARAMIS

Ah! Ah! He is your nephew! He is the monk—and he is the son of milady.

DE WINTER

Alas, yes.

ARAMIS

Wait a while.

(he takes a rifle and aims it at Mordaunt)

GRIMAUD

Fire!

ATHOS

(pushing the rifle aside)

What are you doing, friend?

ARAMIS

The devil take you! I had him right in my sights. I'd have put my ball right through his breast.

ATHOS

It's enough to have killed the mother.

(The Bark begins to move out.)

MORDAUNT

Ah—it's really you! It's really you, gentlemen! I recognize you now and we will meet again in England.

(The Bark disappears—he follows it a moment with his eyes.)

MORDAUNT

Oh, it's Providence that has made me recognize them—it's Providence that has brought them there where I am all powerful—two of the four—will always be there—we won't despair of finding the other two.

(Porthos and D'Artagnan enter.)

PORTHOS

Decidedly, I believe we are late.

D'ARTAGNAN

It's your fault, my dear boy, with your boundless appetite—we will never finish.

PORTHOS

It's not me, it's that clown of a Mousqueton who's always hungry—Mousqueton—have you the provisions?

MOUSQUETON

Yes, Baron.

MORDAUNT

Ah! Ah! It seems to me that our two gentlemen are here.

D'ARTAGNAN

Where the devil are we going to find our Mordaunt now?

PORTHOS

On the jetty. Didn't he give us a rendezvous there?

D'ARTAGNAN

Yes, but at exactly at eight o'clock.

PORTHOS

Eh—well eight o'clock is just striking.

MORDAUNT

Yes, gentlemen, I am very reassured to see you are punctual.

D'ARTAGNAN

It's a military custom that dates back twenty years, sir.

MORDAUNT

I congratulate you on it. Nothing stops us from leaving does it?

D'ARTAGNAN

When you wish, we are ready.

PORTHOS

A moment, sir. Is the ship sufficiently provided?

MORDAUNT

Yes, sir, besides we have only a three-day crossing.

PORTHOS

In three days one can get very hungry.

MORDAUNT

Be easy, gentlemen—and if you have no other objection to make....

D'ARTAGNAN

None at all.

MORDAUNT

Then go on board.

D'ARTAGNAN

Come Porthos.

(Porthos and D'Artagnan cross the plank.)

MOUSQUETON

What sir, must I go up there?

PORTHOS

Without doubt.

D'ARTAGNAN

We are indeed ready.

MOUSQUETON

Ah, you are something else too—you are very brave.

D'ARTAGNAN

Come on, come on.

PORTHOS

Give me you hand, my poor Mousqueton—ah—you're getting old.

(Mousqueton goes on board.)

(Mordaunt in the foreground.)

MORDAUNT

Well Captain André, this lady....

ANDRÉ

She's already there, sir.

MORDAUNT

Bring her here.

ANDRÉ

Right away.

(at the door of the little house)

Come, madam.

MORDAUNT

Put all in readiness for departure. We've got to be out of port before nine o'clock.

QUEEN

(dressed as a Scotswoman)

Sir, they tell me you are the captain of this boat.

MORDAUNT

Not exactly, Madame, but I've rented it.

QUEEN

Then you're the master. And that's whom I wish to speak to.

MORDAUNT

A little closer. What do you wish, madam?

QUEEN

You would render me a great service by giving passage to me and my brother.

MORDAUNT

You're going to England?

QUEEN

To Scotland.

MORDAUNT

But we are going to Newcastle.

QUEEN

I know it, Sir, but from Newcastle, I hope to easily go to County of Perth.

MORDAUNT

It's with great pleasure, Madam but we have only one place free.

QUEEN

Ah, my God, what do you tell me, sir!

MORDAUNT

The truth.

QUEEN

My brother has the greatest wish to accompany me, sir, and he will stay—never mind what place—with the sailors—with the servants.

MORDAUNT

Impossible.

QUEEN

Sir—neither prayers nor money?

MORDAUNT

Nothing.

QUEEN

Then, I must be resigned. I will go alone, sir.

MORDAUNT

In that case, madam, don't lose any time.

QUEEN

(to Parry)

Goodbye, my poor Parry. We must separate. I am going to Newcastle—and from there I will reach the camp of the King where he must be. Get to England by your first opportunity and we will rejoin each other.

PARRY

Oh, madam, to leave Your Majesty.

QUEEN

It must be, my friend.

PARRY

Ah—Your Majesty has called me.

QUEEN

Her friend, some servants like you Parry—worth much more as friends. Those we know.

PARRY

(almost at her knees and kissing her robe)

Ah! Madame!

MORDAUNT

She is the Queen just as I thought. Come on, come on, heaven is delivering them all to me.

(to the Queen)

Will you take my arm madame? They're only waiting for us.

(Noise of all the commands for setting sail. The curtain falls the moment the Queen crosses the plank leading to the boat.)

CURTAIN

ACT II

Scene 4

The largest room in a house in Newcastle occupied by Cromwell.

CROMWELL

And you were saying, Colonel?

GROSLOW

I say, Mr. Cromwell that if you wish it, today or tomorrow, at the latest—King Charles is ours.

CROMWELL

And how's that—let's see, Colonel?

GROSLOW

Because the aid which he's expecting from France is failing him—because in place of an army and treasure which his friend de Winter is to bring him, his friend de Winter brings him nothing but diamonds, the last resources of Madame Henriette, and brings two gentlemen—the last aid, I will not say that the kingdom of France sends him to help him keep his crown, but that the nobility sends to see him die.

CROMWELL

It's good, Colonel. I will think of what you've told me and in my first dispatch, I will advise Parliament of your zeal.

GROSLOW

But general, it seems to me that in your place—

CROMWELL

Sir, I expect news from France, also. I have sent someone to Cardinal Mazarin.

GROSLOW

Your envoy may be too late, general. The waves and the winds take orders from no one—and the time is lacking.

CROMWELL

You deceive yourself, sir—the waves and winds are at the order of the Eternal One. It's for this they call him the God of Tempests—and the Eternal one is for us.

GROSLOW

General—

CROMWELL

(sitting down)

Look out that window.

GROSLOW

Yes, sir.

CROMWELL

It gives on the harbor doesn't it?

GROSLOW

Yes.

CROMWELL

Well—do you see anything new in the port?

GROSLOW

A ship has just come to anchor.

CROMWELL

And on the road from the harbor, can you anyone be seen?

GROSLOW

Two men wrapped in capes—and who appear to be strangers.

CROMWELL

Now listen—what do you hear?

GROSLOW

Someone's coming up.

CROMWELL

The ship that's in the port is the Brig—*The Parliament*—these two men are en route—they are the envoys of Mazarin. This man coming up...

(there's a knocking on the door)

...and who is knocking—is my secretary Mr. Mordaunt. If you doubt it, Colonel—go open and you will see.

GROSLOW

(going to open)

You are truly inspired, sir.

(Enter Mordaunt.)

CROMWELL

Be welcome, Mordaunt! Something told me last night you wold be here this morning.

MORDAUNT

It was the voice of the Lord—the Lord speaks to those who are charged to speak in his name.

CROMWELL

What did you bring from France, my son?

MORDAUNT

Some rich news, sir.

CROMWELL

Be twice welcome then! Have you seen the Cardinal?

MORDAUNT

I have seen him.

CROMWELL

And he gave you a reply?

MORDAUNT

Yes.

CROMWELL

Verbal?

MORDAUNT

Written.

CROMWELL

He sent it with you?

MORDAUNT

So that it would carry more weight with you he sent it by a Lieutenant of the King's Musketeers and by a Lord of the Court.

CROMWELL

Are they named?

MORDAUNT

The Lieutenant—Monsieur le Chevalier d'Artagnan, the Lord Monsieur du Vallon.

CROMWELL

Two spies that he accredits to me.

MORDAUNT

The Genius of the Eternal One is with you sir. They cannot spy on God.

CROMWELL

And those two men are below?

MORDAUNT

They await your orders.

CROMWELL

You hear Colonel Groslow? I believe that the moment you wish for has come.

GROSLOW

What are your commands, general?

CROMWELL

Put the ironsides under arms—order your regiment to be ready at the first sound of a trumpet, and let it be thus with the entire Army.

GROSLOW

I obey.

CROMWELL

In passing, tell those two gentlemen to come up.

(Groslow leaves.)

CROMWELL

You have still something else to tell me, my son?

MORDAUNT

Yes, sir—I have to tell you that on the same boat with us a woman is crossing to England.

CROMWELL

A woman! Who is this woman?

MORDAUNT

The General Cromwell will see her. A chief ought always to see for himself.

CROMWELL

And where will I see her?

MORDAUNT

I've ordered her to be watched and at the moment when—she attempts to leave the city, they will bring her to your Honor.

CROMWELL

You believe, then, this woman is of some importance?

MORDAUNT

You will judge.

CROMWELL

Silence! They're coming.

(Enter D'Artagnan and Porthos.)

MORDAUNT

Come in Gentlemen, you are before General Cromwell.

CROMWELL

Mr. Mordaunt, if you are not too fatigued by your voyage—?

MORDAUNT

I am never fatigued, sir, you know it.

CROMWELL

In that case, take this letter, prepared for you—read it, execute it, at the moment the conditions obtain—after reading it, burn it.

MORDAUNT

Whatever may be the order contained in this letter, it will be carried out, milord.

CROMWELL

Silence, my son! We are not alone.

D'ARTAGNAN

(while Cromwell follows Mordaunt's eyes)

Well, what do you say of that, Porthos?

PORTHOS

Of whom?

D'ARTAGNAN

Of General Cromwell?

PORTHOS

I say he has the manners of the butcher he is.

D'ARTAGNAN

You are mistaken, it is Colonel Harrison who is a butcher.

PORTHOS

Ah, yes, him—he is—

D'ARTAGNAN

(seeing that Cromwell returns)

He is—he is the General Oliver Cromwell. Let me do the talking.

(Mordaunt leaves.)

CROMWELL

Welcome, Gentlemen. I cannot believe what Mordaunt told me.

D'ARTAGNAN

He only told you the truth, sir, if he told you we came to you as envoys of the illustrious Cardinal.

CROMWELL

You will pardon me, but I cannot believe such an honor. The name of the poor Brewer of Huntington is known at the other side of the strait.

PORTHOS

(to himself)

Ah! It's true—he was a brewer.

D'ARTAGNAN

Hush!

(aloud)

It's not the name of the Brewer of Huntington that is known on the other side of the channel sir—it's the name of the conqueror of Marston-Moor and of Newberry.

PORTHOS

Bravo! This devil of a D'Artagnan where does he learn all he says?

CROMWELL

One sees, sir, that you come form the most courteous court in Europe. How was the Queen on your departure?

D'ARTAGNAN

The Queen Anne of Austria?

CROMWELL

No—our queen, Her Majesty Henriette of France, wife of King Charles, whom the faithful children of England regret having to combat at the moment.

D'ARTAGNAN

But I believe Her Majesty is well—it's a long time since I've had the honor of seeing her.

CROMWELL

She no longer comes to the Palace Royal?

D'ARTAGNAN

I don't know if she comes there but it's more than a year since I have seen her.

CROMWELL

Then Cardinal Mazarin goes to pay her his court?

D'ARTAGNAN

Cardinal Mazarin has not the time—he must write and that reminds me that I am bearer of a letter.

CROMWELL

For me, it is true?

D'ARTAGNAN

For you, sir.

CROMWELL

Give it here.

(aside)

Come on, Monsieur de Mazarin chooses his men well. This Chevalier D'Artagnan is a man of wit.

PORTHOS

(low to D'Artagnan)

Say, D'Artagnan.

D'ARTAGNAN

What?

PORTHOS

He doesn't appear very strong to me and can you see how he is dressed?

D'ARTAGNAN

He was even worse dressed when he presented himself to the House of Commons and the famous Hampden said, seeing him—"You see this peasant so poorly dressed. He will be, if I don't deceive myself, one of the greatest men of our times."

PORTHOS

And who is he—the famous Hampden?

D'ARTAGNAN

He was the first man in England before Cromwell made him the second.

CROMWELL

(after having read)

Thanks gentlemen. I have found Monsieur de Mazarin just as I expected him. Mazarin is a grand politician.

PORTHOS

Really, that's funny. No one says so of him in France.

D'ARTAGNAN

And will you do us the honor of entrusting us with a reply, sir?

CROMWELL

You must be fatigued, gentlemen, take some rest first—and tomorrow.

D'ARTAGNAN

You will give us a letter, general?

CROMWELL

No—tomorrow you will leave and you will say—you will say simply what you have seen.

D'ARTAGNAN

Well, what do you say, Porthos?

PORTHOS

I say he did well to give us our leave. I am very hungry.

CROMWELL

My house is yours, gentlemen, and while you stay in England short or long term, you can freely enter and by doing so you do me honor and pleasure.

(Exit Porthos and D'Artagnan)

CROMWELL

(alone)

Come, everything's going my way—all points to success—Mazarin abandons him—and the Scotch sell him. A single man stands between me and the throne—this man is going to disappear—yes—but to take his place—a ghost—let's see—considering everything—is it in my interest that Charles Stuart fall into the abyss and die falling— Once delivered of its King, will England need its General? Isn't it Stuart who makes Cromwell necessary—and Stuart in falling— won't he pull Cromwell down with him? Yes that might be if there were someone in England who could get rid of Cromwell as Cromwell got rid of Stuart. But could Harrison do it? Could Pride, could Fairfax? These instruments, these machines to which I have given the impetus, these automatons on whom I have impressed movement—the Parliament—yes I know it well—there is opposition. It's a blow to strike—that's all—I will smash Parliament. The monarchy is three centuries older than the Parliament and I have already broken the Monarchy—but what have the English left of monarchy?— is it the monarchy or the King they have left? It's the King. Is it even the King?—it's the name. One must find a name which has never been used before. Consul—one must have the virtues of a Brutus.—Dictator?—one mustn't have the vices of a Sulla.—I want a title which permits me to obtain all the honors without imposing any—it must seem to protect England although England has no need of a protector—Well but, "Protector". There's a name—there's a title—there's an unheard of name—new—simple—but haughty at the same time. Which one could indifferently be called—Sir— Milord—Highness.—Divided in parts to come in passing to the Bourgeois, among the commoners, in the Army. I've made my route a triple station long enough to know the bourgeois, the parliamentarians, and the soldiers—there remains only the nobility for me to study. Bah! The nobility they will be at my feet when I am Protector. What does it ask? Not to be conquered but to make it seem that it is not I or it that has killed its King. Well, I've played this role right up to the present and have only to continue. Charles Stuart himself doesn't regard me as his enemy—and often takes me as intermediary between him and the Parliament. Intermediary…

(with a smile)

…as the hatchet is an intermediary between the executioner and the condemned. Ah! Someone—Protector is decidedly an excellent title. Whom comes there?

(Enter two soldiers with the Queen disguised as at Boulogne.)

SOLDIER

General, there is a woman—

CROMWELL

Ah, yes, I had forgotten. Who is this woman?

SOLDIER

A woman arrived on the ship *The Parliament* and whom we stopped as she attempted to pass into the royalist camp—and we brought her to you.

CROMWELL

Fine, my friends, bring her in.

SOLDIER

(to the wings)

Do you hear? The General calls you.

QUEEN

(entering)

The General—what General gentlemen?

SOLDIER

There's only one general in all England—not all who bear the title— but the only one who merits the title. It is General Cromwell.

QUEEN

It is then from General Cromwell that I must ask justice for the violence that has been done me?

CROMWELL

Yes, madam, it is General Cromwell who will accord you justice—be certain of it.

QUEEN

There was violence sir. If English law still guarantees liberty to all.

CROMWELL

The English law guarantees liberty to all good Englishmen.

QUEEN

But, where are the good Englishmen? Are they in the camp of General Oliver Cromwell? Are they in the camp of King Charles?

CROMWELL

There are good Englishmen everywhere, madam.

QUEEN

Even among those who make war on their sovereign?

CROMWELL

We don't make war against our sovereign, we make war against his ministers. We make war on Strafford, on Laud, on Windebank— We respect the monarchy in the King, the King in the man— Now— who are you?

QUEEN

I am Catherine Parry.

CROMWELL

Where are you going?

QUEEN

To Scotland.

CROMWELL

To what end?

QUEEN

To preserve, in the name of my brother and myself, the inheritance of my father who has just died.

CROMWELL

You are then of County Perth?

QUEEN

Yes.

CROMWELL

You are then the daughter of William Parry?

QUEEN

Yes.

CROMWELL

You are then the sister of John Parry?

QUEEN

Yes. How do you know that?

CROMWELL

I know it, as you can see. Why didn't you say all this to those who arrested you?

QUEEN

I did say it.

CROMWELL

And they did not believe you?

QUEEN

No!

CROMWELL

What do you expect? They have been so often deceived that they have become suspicious?

SOLDIER

This woman spoke the truth then, general?

CROMWELL

Yes.

SOLDIER

Then we did wrong to arrest her and bring her to you?

CROMWELL

No it's for me to weed the good from the bad. It's for this that the Eternal One has made me as I am.

SOLDIER

Then she can pass freely?

CROMWELL

Freely—Go.

(they Leave)

QUEEN

Then I can follow them?

CROMWELL

(rising and revealing himself)

A minute more, if Your Majesty will permit it.

QUEEN

Good heavens! What did you just say, sir?

CROMWELL

I say that it is very imprudent for the daughter of Henry IV and the sister of Louis XIII and the wife of Charles Stuart to come to England at this time and disembark in a city held by General Oliver Cromwell.

QUEEN

You are deceived, sir. I am neither daughter, nor sister, nor wife of a King. I am only the daughter of a poor highlander.

CROMWELL

William Parry has only one son and one daughter.

QUEEN

Well—this daughter.

CROMWELL

This daughter whose name you have taken died six months ago— and your father whose inheritance you seek is alive.

QUEEN

Why, you know everyone in England or Scotland.

CROMWELL

Yes—all those whom it is my interest or my duty to know madam— even when Your Majesty wishes that I did not know it.

QUEEN

Very well, I won't deny it any longer. I am not a Queen who intends
to reign in her Kingdom, for in reality Charles is no longer King—
but only a wife who comes to partake the fate of her spouse. Now do
with me what you wish.

CROMWELL

It's for me to await the orders of my sovereign.

QUEEN

What are you saying?

CROMWELL

I say that, for my colleague, for the Parliament, for the nation—
Charles the First is perhaps no more than Charles Stuart—but for
me—Charles Stuart is always King. Yes, madam, and you will tell
him what you are going to hear from my mouth and what you have
not heard from anybody—the truth! You will tell him that if he
gives battle, he is lost.

QUEEN

But Parliament—.

CROMWELL

You will tell him that if he treats with the Parliament he is lost.

QUEEN

My God!

CROMWELL

You will tell him that in all England perhaps, at this time, there's
only one man who sincerely desires the health of King Charles—and
that this man is General Oliver Cromwell.

QUEEN

Do you speak frankly, Sir?

CROMWELL

Yes, but let him be careful—behind my will there is Destiny. Behind Providence there is a fatality—and I, madame, I am the man of destiny the man of fatality. Let him leave!

QUEEN

But that would be to renounce all hope.

CROMWELL

Madam, at the age of fifteen a woman appeared to me—she held in her hand a crowned head—and she took the crown from that head and put it on mine. Let him leave!

QUEEN

But you admit then—that?

CROMWELL

Madame, my nurse had a spot of blood which ran from her shoulder to her breast, of the type that when giving me suck I had the air of drinking not milk but blood— Let him depart! Let him leave!

QUEEN

He will leave, sir. But how can I get to the King?

CROMWELL

I will give you a safe conduct.

QUEEN

But if I get lost—night is coming on.

CROMWELL

I will give you a guide.

QUEEN

When?

CROMWELL

Right away. Wait—

QUEEN

Ah, sir.

CROMWELL

Take care—if when they enter they think I am doing grace rather than justice—

(writing a few lines)

Here's a pass for a woman going to the Royal Army.

QUEEN

Thanks! Thanks!

CROMWELL

This is not all!

(he strikes his hands).

Findley.

(a servant enters)

Findley—you will accompany madame, under whatever costume it pleases you to take to the outskirts of the royalist camp.

FINDLEY

Yes, general.

CROMWELL

Something that she may wish to offer you, you will not accept.

FINDLEY

No, general.

CROMWELL

It will take you two hours to get to camp.

(Findley makes a movement)

You hear—two hours—not more, not less.

FINDLEY

Right, general.

CROMWELL

(to Queen)

Now I hope you will no longer say to those whom I am sending you, I am your enemy.

QUEEN

God watch that—you speak the truth, sir, while waiting, thanks.

(The Queen leaves with Findley.)

CROMWELL

In two hours, it will be too late for Charles to profit from this advice—but the advice will have been given at least.

BLACKOUT

ACT II

Scene 5

The Camp of King Charles—at night, the royal tent decorated by a large tapestry with the arms of England and Scotland. At the left, a house whose first floor is shut by a window decorated with bars of iron and a door to which one gets by three steps. The window is up at left. In the center—countryside with plains and mountains.

(De Winter is sitting on his cloak before the entrance to the King's tent.)

ARAMIS

(to a Sentinel)

And you say, my friend, that for two years you haven't been paid?

SENTINEL

No sir—and it's hard with a war such as we are waging.

ARAMIS

Yes, I know it well—but then, when King Charles regains his throne he will reward his faithful Scots.

SENTINEL

Yes—if he regains it.

ARAMIS

We hope that God will give the advantage to the just cause.

ATHOS

(coming rapidly from behind the house)

Aramis!

ARAMIS

Well?

ATHOS

Not an instant to lose. We must warn the King.

ARAMIS

What's happening then?

ATHOS

It would take too long to tell you— Where is de Winter?

ARAMIS

Come!

(giving a half pistole to the sentinel).

Here my friend. Here's a half pistole to drink the King's health.

SENTINEL

How welcome it is— It's a long time since I have seen the like—the last that passed through my hands.

ATHOS

(touching de Winter on the shoulder)

De Winter! De Winter!

DE WINTER

(awakening)

Ah, it's you, Count. It's you, Chevalier. Have you remarked how red the sun is setting this evening?

ATHOS

Milord in a position as precarious as ours—it's the earth we must look to not the heavens—have you studied our Scotch?

DE WINTER

Which Scotch?

ATHOS

Eh! By God—ours—the Scots of Count de Loeven.

DE WINTER

No.

ATHOS

Do you believe in their fidelity?

DE WINTER

Without doubt.

(one hears the march of a patrol)

See with what regularity the service is performed

(one hears the hour strike in the distance).

Seven o'clock and the hour sounds—that's the relief of the sentinels.

ATHOS

Right.

(The sentinels are relieved successively—then a patrol approaches from King Charles tent)

SENTINEL

Who goes?—

MORDAUNT

(at the head of the Patrol)

Charles and loyalty. The countersign?

SENTINEL

Not to let any approach the tent of the King except those who have the password.

MORDAUNT

(giving a purse to the Sentinel)

Here—there's what was promised.

ATHOS

(who has heard)

Money!

DE WINTER

(to Aramis while Athos takes a few steps to be sure the patrol has gone off).

Tell me, Chevalier, isn't it a tradition in France that the watch saw spots of blood on the board the day Henry IV was assassinated playing checkers with M. de Bassompierre?

ARAMIS

Yes, milord—and the Marshall many times told me the story himself in my youth.

DE WINTER

That's it—and the next day Henry IV was killed.

ARAMIS

What brings this vision to your memory, count?

DE WINTER

Nothing—only you know, chevalier, that the strongest of men are not masters of themselves in hours of sadness—but let's speak no more of that. Count, you had something to tell me.

ATHOS

I wanted to speak to the King.

DE WINTER

After having worked all day, the King is sleeping.

ATHOS

Milord, I have to reveal to him things of the greatest importance.

DE WINTER

These things cannot be put off until tomorrow?

ATHOS

It's necessary for him to know instantly—perhaps it is already too late.

DE WINTER

(raising the curtain of the King's tent)

Then enter, count.

(By the light of a lamp one sees a table covered with papers. The King is sleeping, resting on the table.)

ATHOS

(sighing)

Sire!

KING

(awakening)

Is it you, Count?

ATHOS

Yes, sire.

KING

You wake me. While I was sleeping—and you bring me some news—

ATHOS

Alas, yes, Your Majesty has divined correctly.

KING

Then the news is bad.

ATHOS

Yes, sire.

KING

No matter! The messenger is welcome—and you cannot come to me without giving me pleasure—you whose devotion knows no country and resists misfortune. You who were sent to me by my good Henriette, may God make her more happy there than I am here! Speak then with confidence, Sir.

ATHOS

Sire, Cromwell came to Newcastle yesterday.

KING

I know it.

ATHOS

Your Majesty knows why he has come?

KING

To fight me.

ATHOS

To purchase you.

KING

Who told you that, count?

ATHOS

I say, sire, that the Scotch Army is owed 400,000 pounds sterling.

KING

For pay arrears, yes—for the least two years my brave and faithful Scots fought for honor alone.

ATHOS

Well sire, while honor may be a beautiful thing, they are tired of battling for it—and this evening....

KING

And this evening?

ATHOS

This evening they sold Your Majesty for 200,000 pounds sterling— that is to say, for half their pay.

DE WINTER

What's he saying!

ARAMIS

I doubt it.

KING

The Scotch have sold me—impossible! The Scotch sell their King for 200,000 pounds?

ATHOS

The Jews sold their God for thirty pieces of silver.

KING

And who is the Judas that has taken this step?

ATHOS

The Count de Loeven.

KING

And to whom has he done it?

ATHOS

With the Secretary of M. Cromwell.

DE WINTER

With Mordaunt?

ATHOS

Yes, Milord.

KING

Isn't he the young man who pursued me with such bitterness, de Winter?

DE WINTER

Alas, yes.

KING

What have I done to him? I don't recall.

DE WINTER

At my request, Your Majesty declared him a bastard—and forbade him to pretend to the wealth or the name of his father.

KING

Ah—that's true. But it was justice and I don't repent of it.

(to Athos)

You were saying then, Count?

ATHOS

I say that sleeping near the tent of de Loeven I heard all—saw all.

KING

And when will this odious step be consummated?

ATHOS

This very night! As Your Majesty can see, there's no time to lose.

KING

No time to lose! To do what? Since you say I've been sold.

ATHOS

To profit by the night, sire, to cross the Tyne, to rejoin Lord Montrose—who will not sell you.

KING

And what can I do in Scotland? A guerrilla war! Count, such a war is unworthy of a King.

ATHOS

The example of Robert the Bruce is there to absolve you, Sir.

KING

No, Count, no. I've struggled too long. I am at the end of my strength. They have sold me—let them deliver me, and let the shame of their treason fall on them.

ATHOS

Sire, perhaps it is thus a King ought to speak but this is not the way a husband and a father should act—Sire, we have crossed the sea—Sire, we came in the name of your wife and children, I say to you, "Come Sire—God wishes it!"

KING

You've convinced me, Count—what do you advise me to do?

ATHOS

Sir—does Your Majesty have in the entire army a single regiment on which you can count?

KING

De Winter—do you believe in the fidelity of yours?

DE WINTER

Sire—they are only men—and these men have become weak and bad—I believe in their fidelity—but I cannot answer for it—I would trust them with my life, but I hesitate to trust Your Majesty's to them.

ATHOS

Eh! Count only on us—then—we are three men, devoted, and resolute—we will suffer. Let Your Majesty take hope in the midst of us and we will cross the Tyne, gain Scotland and we are saved.

KING

Is that your advice, de Winter?

DE WINTER

Yes, sire.

KING

Is it yours, M. d'Herblay?

ARAMIS

Yes, sire.

KING

Then let it be as you desire. Let's go.

ATHOS

Wait, Sire.

KING

What then?

ATHOS

The sentinels who watch at Your Majesty's door—can give the alarm seeing you leave—they must be removed.

KING

The sentinels?

ATHOS

Sire, I saw the officer who placed them where they are count them out money.

KING

Oh! My God!

DE WINTER

And how to relieve them?

ATHOS

Have you but four men on whom you can count, Milord?

DE WINTER

Yes, but they are my own servants.

ATHOS

Go take them and do it.

DE WINTER

I am going.

(he leaves the tent)

ARAMIS

And the rest of us, Count. What shall we do in the meantime?

KING

Come, Gentlemen, I will find something for you to do.

(King goes to an armoire; he pulls out two plaques of the Order of the Garter)

ATHOS

What are you doing, Sire?

KING

On your knees, Count.

ATHOS

Sire, these orders cannot be for us.

KING

And why is that?

ATHOS

They are almost royal.

KING

Pass in review all the Kings of the World, my brothers—who in this crisis abandon me and find me greater hearts than yours—! No, no, Gentlemen—you don't do yourselves justice—but that's my concern—to your knees, Count.

ATHOS

You command it, Sire.

KING

(drawing sword)

I want to say to you, "I am going to make you a Knight, be brave, faithful and loyal". I say to you "you are brave, faithful and loyal—I am going to make you a Knight. In your turn, M. D'Herblay.

(Aramis falls to his knees at the same moment de Winter appears center with his four men.)

SENTINEL

Who goes there?

DE WINTER

Charles and loyalty.

SENTINEL

Advance.

ARAMIS

(rising)

Thanks, sire.

ATHOS

(extending his hands toward the Sentinels)

Listen!

(During this time, de Winter and his men are disarming one of the sentinels but the other one who has heard the noise puts his pike on guard).

2ND SENTINEL

Who goes there?

ARAMIS

(who has left the tent from the rear—putting his dagger on his breast)

If you say a word, you are dead.

ATHOS

(to de Winter's men)

Take the two sentinels and hide them from sight.

ARAMIS

And—at the first word, the first gesture, the first sign they make of giving the alarm—kill them!

DE WINTER

Now, Sire, we are ready.

(They take the two Sentinels away)

KING

We must flee then!

ATHOS

To flee across an army, Sire, in all countries of the world—it's known as charging.

KING

Let's go then, gentlemen.

DE WINTER

(to Aramis)

Is one of us wounded? I see drops of blood on the ground.

ATHOS

(who has already taken several steps outside)

Listen, sire, listen.

KING

What's wrong?

ATHOS

I hear the tramping of a large troupe and the neighing of horses.

ARAMIS

It's too late, we are surrounded.

(De Winter takes two steps forward, while the two companions and the King listen; then he returns.)

DE WINTER

It's the enemy.

KING

Then, all is lost!

ATHOS

There is still a way, sire.

KING

What?

ATHOS

That Your Majesty, instead of keeping his well-known costume, take one from one of us and give us his while they pursue the one who takes the King's—perhaps the King will be able to escape.

ARAMIS

The advice is good, sire—and if Your Majesty will indeed do one of us this honor.

KING

What do you think of this advice, de Winter?

DE WINTER

I think that if there is a way in the world of saving you, the Count de la Fère has just proposed it.

KING

But it is certain death or at least prison for whoever takes my place.

DE WINTER

It is an honor to have saved his King—choose, sire.

KING

Come, de Winter.

DE WINTER

Oh! Thank you, my King!

ATHOS

It is just—he has served him much longer than we have.

ARAMIS

Hurry, sire—we will protect the entrance to your tent.

(While these two place themselves as sentinels—sword in hand, the King gives de Winter his Cordon of Saint Esprit, his hat and his doublet—in exchange de Winter gives the King the same objects plus his armor. At the moment the exchange terminates and the King leaves by the rear of the tent—a patrol composed of ten men appears.)

ARAMIS

Who goes there?

ATHOS

Who goes there?

D'ARTAGNAN

(to Mordaunt)

Singular country of yours, sir, where one always draws one's purse and never one's sword.

PORTHOS

It appears to be the custom in England.

MORDAUNT

By sword or by gold—what's the difference, gentlemen?—you see the camp is ours.

D'ARTAGNAN

It is equal. What a strange war.

ARAMIS & ATHOS

Who goes there, then?

MORDAUNT

Charles and Loyalty.

ARAMIS & ATHOS

You cannot pass.

MORDAUNT

What—why cannot we pass?

D'ARTAGNAN

Finally! This goes wrong in the end—and I begin to believe we will draw swords.

MORDAUNT

Who has changed the password then?

ARAMIS

The king.

MORDAUNT

Why? For what reason?

ATHOS

Because you are traitors.

DE WINTER

Traitors.

PORTHOS

He said traitors, I believe.

D'ARTAGNAN

That's a hard word, gentlemen and we are going, I fear, to ram it down your throat.

ARAMIS

Come here!

MORDAUNT

Fine. Crack heads gentlemen—we are going to the King's tent.

(to his men)

Come!

(Athos fights D'Artagnan, Aramis, Porthos—the four are of equal strength. Suddenly Mordaunt appears in the center of the tent. The men who follow Mordaunt take de Winter and cry "The King, the King! Take him alive!" thinking de Winter is King.)

MORDAUNT

No—it's not the King—no! You deceive yourselves. Right, Milord de Winter—you are not the King—in fact, Milord de Winter, you are my uncle?

D'ARTAGNAN

(recoiling before Mordaunt)

The Avenger!

MORDAUNT

Remember my mother.

(killing de Winter with a pistol shot)

(From the light of the torches the four recognize each other.)

(Aramis, Porthos, D'Artagnan, and Athos take their swords from their left hands to their right)

Musketeers.

D'ARTAGNAN

Surrender, Athos—you surrender to me, but it's not a surrender.

PORTHOS

Aramis, you understand.

ARAMIS

I surrender.

MORDAUNT

(kneeling near the body of de Winter)

Two—

ATHOS

(pointing to Mordaunt)

Do you see this young man?

D'ARTAGNAN

The son of Milady, right?

PORTHOS

The Monk.

ARAMIS

Yes.

D'ARTAGNAN

Don't breathe a word, don't make a gesture—don't risk a look to me or Porthos—for Milady is not dead, and her soul lives in the body of this demon.

(During this time, the King has been surrounded and pushed on stage.)

KING

Which of you will be the first to dare to put a hand on his King?

GROSLOW

(entering)

Charles Stuart, give me your sword.

KING

Colonel Groslow, the King does not surrender—the man cedes to force—that is all—

(breaking his sword)

GROSLOW

Victory, gentlemen! The King is prisoner—we hold the King.

MORDAUNT

(turning)

The King—the King is taken?

SEVERAL VOICES

Yes! Yes!

MORDAUNT

Fine—only that was lacking.

(Mordaunt sees the four men.)

ATHOS

He has seen us.

ARAMIS

Let me kill him.

D'ARTAGNAN

(looking at his friends)

Hang it!

(to Mordaunt)

Fine prize, friend Mordaunt—well taken—and we took each of us—
M. du Vallon and I—Knights of the Garter and none other.

MORDAUNT

But these are French, it seems to me.

D'ARTAGNAN

French.

ATHOS

I am.

D'ARTAGNAN

Well—they are prisoners of compatriots.

KING

(to Athos and Aramis)

Your health, gentlemen. The night was unfortunate—but it's not your fault, God be thanked—where is my old de Winter?

MORDAUNT

Look for him with Strafford!

KING

(seeing the corpse)

Then—like Strafford, he has paid the price of his fidelity.

(kneeling before de Winter, raising his head and embracing his face)

Adieu faithful heart, gone above to find the reward for devotion—and to prepare my call of martyrdom. Adieu.

D'ARTAGNAN

De Winter is dead?

ATHOS

Yes—by his nephew.

D'ARTAGNAN

It's the first of us to go. May he sleep in peace. He was a brave man.

KING

Now, gentlemen, take me where you wish.

GROSLOW

The order of General Cromwell is to take you to London.

KING

When must I leave?

GROSLOW

Instantly.

KING

Let's get on with it, then.

ATHOS

(to the King who is leaving)

Health to fallen Majesty.

D'ARTAGNAN

'Sdeath! Athos you will get us all strangled.

(The King leaves with Groslow.)

MORDAUNT

(to D'Artagnan)

Will you come to the General's home, gentlemen—he has some compliments to pay you.

D'ARTAGNAN

With great pleasure, sire. But it's necessary for us first to put our prisoners in some secure place. Do you know, sir, that each of these gentlemen is worth two thousand pistoles?

MORDAUNT

Oh, be easy—my soldiers will guard them—and guard them well. I will answer for them.

D'ARTAGNAN

I wouldn't wish to give them the trouble and I will guard them better myself— Besides, what does it matter? A good room secured with bars as here for example or their simple word that they will not flee. For in our country the oath is worth the game—says a proverb. I am going to put order to this, sir—after that I will have the honor of presenting myself to the general and asking from him his orders to return to France.

MORDAUNT

You plan then on leaving soon?

D'ARTAGNAN

Our mission is finished and nothing further keeps us in England except the pleasure of the great man to whom we have been sent.

MORDAUNT

Fine, Gentlemen.

(to a sergeant)

Sergeant Harry, take ten men with you and guard this door and under no pretext let these two prisoners leave.

SERGEANT

And the other two?

MORDAUNT

They are free—now, do you know this house?

SERGEANT

I've commanded a post here.

MORDAUNT

Is there another way out of here?

SERGEANT

No.

MORDAUNT

They cannot flee?

SERGEANT

Impossible.

MORDAUNT

Good—do you know where General Cromwell is?

(leaving)

My horse! My horse!

(During this time, D'Artagnan has made the two friends enter the house. He's closed the door and put the key in his pocket. Porthos watches him.)

D'ARTAGNAN

Friend Porthos, while I am religiously guarding the sill of this door, you are going to do me the pleasure— Come close so these two co-medians here don't hear what we are saying— You are going to do me the pleasure of reuniting Grimaud, Mousqueton, and Blaisois.

PORTHOS

That's easy. I have indicated to them a place where they must oc-cupy themselves preparing supper for us.

D'ARTAGNAN

Good! We will eat tomorrow afternoon. Go find them, Porthos—let them hold our horses ready for any eventuality behind this house.

PORTHOS

Why not sleep here?

D'ARTAGNAN

Because the air is unhealthy.

PORTHOS

Bah!

D'ARTAGNAN

It's as I have the honor of telling you.

PORTHOS

Then—that's another matter.

(He goes off. D'Artagnan is alone on the highest step)

D'ARTAGNAN

Now, let's see what these clowns are doing.

(he descends a step, then addresses himself to Sergeant Harry and his men who are established before the house).

My friends, would you like something?

SERGEANT

No, sir.

D'ARTAGNAN

There, why are you staying there, if you please?

SERGEANT

Because we have orders to help you guard the prisoners.

D'ARTAGNAN

Truly—and who has given you that order?

SERGEANT

Mr. Mordaunt.

D'ARTAGNAN

I recognize his delicate attention—here, my friend.

SERGEANT

What's that?

D'ARTAGNAN

A half-crown, my friend, to drink the health of Mr. Mordaunt.

SERGEANT

Puritans don't drink.

(he puts the coin in his pocket)

PORTHOS

(reappearing)

It's done.

D'ARTAGNAN

Silence!

PORTHOS

I haven't said anything as to what was done.

D'ARTAGNAN

It would be better—wait Porthos, go in and don't leave until you hear me drum on the door—the March of the Musketeers.

PORTHOS

Fine—I'll go in—but you—what are you doing here?

D'ARTAGNAN

Me? Nothing—I watch the moon.

(Exit Porthos)

(Cromwell slowly enters the tent in the distance.)

CROMWELL

This tent has two doors. An exit which leads to the scaffold—and an entrance by which I came in and which leads me to a throne—Here I am where he was— Perhaps I will go where he's going? Proud Charles Stuart—who would have said—ten years ago, a month ago—an hour ago—that on this table with this paper prepared for you—with this pen that you have dipped in ink—that I would write to all the Kings of Europe "Charles Stuart is no longer your brother". Let's write.

(Mordaunt appears at the door to the right. With a slight movement of impatience)

I told you I wished to be alone.

MORDAUNT

I didn't think that this applied to one you called your son, yet if you order it, I am ready to leave.

CROMWELL

Ah, it's you, Mordaunt. Since you're here, that's fine—remain.

MORDAUNT

I bring you my congratulations, sir.

CROMWELL

Your congratulations—about what?

MORDAUNT

On the taking of Charles Stuart—you are now master of England.

CROMWELL

I was much better off two hours ago.

MORDAUNT

How so, general?

CROMWELL

Two hours ago, England needed me to capture the tyrant. Now the tyrant is captured. They tell me the Colonel of the Regiment of the Guards of Charles Stuart—who was wearing the king's clothes was killed.

MORDAUNT

Yes, sir.

CROMWELL

By whom?

MORDAUNT

By me.

CROMWELL

What was his name?

MORDAUNT

Lord de Winter.

CROMWELL

He was your uncle.

MORDAUNT

The traitors to England are not of my family.

CROMWELL

(with melancholy)

Mordaunt, you are a terrible servant.

MORDAUNT

When heaven orders—one can only march with its orders.

CROMWELL

(bowing)

You are the strongest of the strong, Mordaunt. Go.

MORDAUNT

Before my leaving, sir—I have some questions to address to you and a demand to make of you, my master.

CROMWELL

To me?

MORDAUNT

To you!

(bowing)

I come to you, my hero, my protector, my father—and I ask you—Master—are you satisfied with me?

CROMWELL

(looking at him with astonishment)

Without doubt, for since I have known you, you have done not only your duty but more than your duty. You have been a faithful friend, adroit negotiator—good soldier—but what are you leading up to?

MORDAUNT

To tell you Milord, that the moment is come where you can, by a single word, reward me for all my services.

CROMWELL

Ah! It's true, sir—I forgot that all your services deserve its reward. That you have served me and not yet been rewarded.

MORDAUNT

Sir, I am being so, at this instant, even in the midst of my wishes.

CROMWELL

How's that?

MORDAUNT

Sir, will you grant my request?

CROMWELL

Let's see first if it is possible.

MORDAUNT

When you have had a desire and you have charged me with its accomplishment have I ever replied—"What you wish is impossible, sir?"

CROMWELL

Well then, Mordaunt, I promise you to do justice to your demand.

MORDAUNT

Sir, with the King there were two other prisoners. I ask them of you.

CROMWELL

English?

MORDAUNT

French.

CROMWELL

They are then offering a considerable ransom.

MORDAUNT

I'm not concerned if they have offered a ransom.

CROMWELL

But they are friends to you?

MORDAUNT

Yes, sir—you have said the word—they are friends to me, and very dear friends—so dear that I will give my life to have theirs.

CROMWELL

Well, Mordaunt, I give them to you; do with them as you wish.

MORDAUNT

Thanks, sir, thanks

(throwing himself to his knees)

My life is henceforth yours and in losing it, I would still be in debt it to you. Thanks, you have paid me magnificently for my services.

CROMWELL

What! No rewards! No titles! No grade promotions!

MORDAUNT

You have given me all that you could give me, milord—and from this day, I absolve you of the rest.

(He rushes toward the tent. To Sergeant)

The prisoners are still there?

SERGEANT

Yes, sir.

MORDAUNT

Take them and conduct them instantly to my lodging.

D'ARTAGNAN

If you please, sir.

MORDAUNT

Ah—you are here.

D'ARTAGNAN

Yes.

MORDAUNT

You have heard, then?

D'ARTAGNAN

Yes—but I don't understand.

MORDAUNT

Sir, I've ordered this man to conduct these prisoners to my lodging.

D'ARTAGNAN

To your lodging? Why did you say that, if you please? Pardon the curiosity, but I would like to know why the prisoners taken by M. du Vallon and M. D'Artagnan ought to be taken to Mr. Mordaunt's residence.

MORDAUNT

Because the prisoners are mine and I can dispose of them to my fantasy.

D'ARTAGNAN

Permit me—you are committing an error—the prisoners belong to those who captured them. You can take your uncle, you have killed him—you were the master—we could kill M. de la Fère and D'Herblay—we have taken them—each to his own taste.

PORTHOS

(hearing from inside)

Oh! Oh!

MORDAUNT

Sir, you are making a useless resistance: these prisoners have been given to me by General Oliver Cromwell.

D'ARTAGNAN

Ah, Mr. Mordaunt—why didn't you begin by telling me that? In truth, you come on the part of Mr. Oliver Cromwell, the illustrious captain?

MORDAUNT

Yes, sir.

D'ARTAGNAN

In that case, I bow—take them.

PORTHOS

Oh! But what has he said then?

MORDAUNT

Thanks.

D'ARTAGNAN

But if General Cromwell, in reality, made a gift to you of our prisoners—he undoubtedly gave a written act of donation—he gave you this little letter for me—a scrap of paper in his name. Kindly show me this letter—and confide scrap of paper to me.

MORDAUNT

When I tell you a thing, sir, do you injure me by doubting it?

D'ARTAGNAN

Me doubt what you say to me, dear Monsieur Mordaunt! God prevent me from it! But you know if I abandon my compatriots, I must have an excuse—after returning to France they can reproach me for having sold them by God! And I must reply to such an accusation by showing the order of Monsieur Cromwell.

MORDAUNT

You're right, sir—you shall have this order.

PORTHOS

What's he saying?

D'ARTAGNAN

But while waiting, let me keep the prisoners.

MORDAUNT

Oh! sir—General Cromwell is there in King Charles' tent. It's a delay of hardly five minutes—that's all.

(He drums on the door of the house with a little stick.)

MORDAUNT

Do you know, sir that I command here?

(Porthos comes out and places himself in the door way)

D'ARTAGNAN

No—I don't know it.

MORDAUNT

And that—if I wish, with ten men—

D'ARTAGNAN

Oh, sir—one sees quite well that you don't know us although we have had the honor of traveling in your company. We are French—we are gentlemen—we are capable, Mr. du Vallon and I of killing you—you and your soldiers. Right, Monsieur du Vallon?

PORTHOS

Yes!

D'ARTAGNAN

By God! Don't be bull-headed, Mr. Mordaunt—for when one is bull-headed, I get bull-headed, too—then I become ferociously head strong, and then M. du Vallon, who in such a case is still more pig headed and more ferocious than I—right, M. du Vallon?

PORTHOS

More pig-headed, and more ferocious, yes, that's the word.

MORDAUNT

Well, then, sir—follow me to him.

D'ARTAGNAN

Oh—I wouldn't dare disturb him. Such familiarities are fine for you who are his secretary, his friend—it's all right for you who he calls his son.

MORDAUNT

Very well. Wait for me there, sir. I am going to him.

D'ARTAGNAN

Well then!

MORDAUNT

Don't lose sight of these two men.

SERGEANT

Be easy.

(Mordaunt goes into the tent.)

MORDAUNT

(to Cromwell)

Sir—

CROMWELL

(writing)

A moment, Mordaunt! I have finished.

D'ARTAGNAN

Friend Porthos, do you still have that pretty little fist which makes you equal to Milo of Croton?

PORTHOS

Always.

D'ARTAGNAN

Can you make, as before, a circle with a bar of iron—and a cork-screw with a handle from fire tongs?

PORTHOS

Certainly.

D'ARTAGNAN

Then go back in—take one of the bars from the window just as it is understand—just as it is.

PORTHOS

It will come out.

D'ARTAGNAN

Then pass through the bars first Athos—then Aramis, and finally yourself.

PORTHOS

Fine. But you?

D'ARTAGNAN

Don't worry about me.

PORTHOS

Fine.

(He goes into the house)

CROMWELL

What do you want, Mordaunt?

MORDAUNT

A written order, sir—the order to take the two prisoners—they refuse to give them to me unless I bring them an order written by your hand.

CROMWELL

But—?

MORDAUNT

Ah! You have promised me these two men, sir— Do you refuse them to me now?

CROMWELL

You are right.

(taking a paper and writing)

MORDAUNT

(from the tent to the Sergeant)

Are they still there?

SERGEANT

Yes.

MORDAUNT

No one budges?

(At this moment, Athos descends from the window.)

SERGEANT

No one.

MORDAUNT

Good.

(Aramis comes out in his turn.)

D'ARTAGNAN

(opening the door partially)

Well?

PORTHOS

It's done.

D'ARTAGNAN

Bravo, Porthos.

CROMWELL

(to Mordaunt)

D'ARTAGNAN

Are you there?

PORTHOS

Yes.

D'ARTAGNAN

My turn now.

(He goes in and shuts the door and locks it)

MORDAUNT

(leaving the tent)

Monsieur D'Artagnan, Monsieur D'Artagnan! Here I am.

(he mounts the steps)

The door is locked.

FINDLEY

(entering the tent)

General—this woman has just arrived in the camp—what shall be done with her?

CROMWELL

She is free to go where she wishes—we don't make war on women.

D'ARTAGNAN

(who has passed by the window)

Servant, M. Mordaunt.

MORDAUNT

Monsieur d'Artagnan! To me, Sergeant, help me force this door.

(They force it. Mordaunt rushes in and sees the bars pulled out)

Ah! To arms! To arms!

CROMWELL

(rising)

What is it?

MORDAUNT

These men—these prisoners—these demons! Escaped! Ah! To arms! To arms!

(He leaves running followed by a crowd of soldiers)

CROMWELL

(to himself)

It was to kill these two men that he asked me for them? What kind of servants have I got?

CURTAIN

ACT III

Scene 6

The Parliament Square—to the left the facade of the Hôtel Staghorn—to the right the entrance to Parliament.

(The People cross the stage.)

PEOPLE

To Parliament! To Parliament!

FINDLEY

(on watch at the door of the Parliament)

No one can enter.

TOM LOWE

Why can't we enter? They refuse to let the people enter Parliament. Comrades! Let's break down the doors.

PEOPLE

Let's break down the doors.

(They force the entrance and pass despite the Guards.)

ATHOS

(leaving the Staghorn with Aramis)

Chevalier—I can's stand by any longer—the people have just entered Parliament—we must see for ourselves.

ARAMIS

D'Artagnan, who never returns?

D'ARTAGNAN

(coming up in the dress of a worker)

Here I am! Here I am! Well, are we ready?

ATHOS

(dressed like one of the people)

Yes, dear friend.

ARAMIS

(dressed like a bourgeois)

No one except Porthos is looking for a mirror. Come on, Porthos!

D'ARTAGNAN

Well—what do you say to the new costumes I have found?

ATHOS

I say we are frightful!

ARAMIS

We must fear the puritans to shiver so!

D'ARTAGNAN

Me, I have a strong with to preach.

PORTHOS

Brrr! I'm cold in the head and this cursed fog has penetrated me to the bone, in despite of this ugly cassock which hides our dress of musketeers.

ATHOS

(to D'Artagnan)

You've come from the sitting?

D'ARTAGNAN

I have.

ATHOS

What did you learn?

D'ARTAGNAN

That the verdict will be given today and that it will be given perhaps any moment.

ATHOS

Who by?

D'ARTAGNAN

The purified Parliament.

ARAMIS

What do you mean, the Purified Parliament? Are there two Parliaments?

D'ARTAGNAN

By the purified Parliament, dear friend, one means the Parliament that Colonel Pride has purified.

ARAMIS

Ah, truly, these people are the most supremely ingenious— D'Artagnan, you must when you return to France, teach these ways to Cardinal Mazarin—as a result of this purification there will be no Parliament at all.

PORTHOS

Who's this Colonel Pride, after all?

D'ARTAGNAN

Colonel Pride, my dear Porthos, is an old carriage driver, a man of great wit who noticed once in driving his cart that when he found a stone on his way, that it was easier to pick up the stone than to pass around it. Of 251 members who compose the Parliament, 191 irritate him, and have been thrown from the political carriage. He took them as he used to take his stone and threw them out of the Chamber.

PORTHOS

Pretty!

D'ARTAGNAN

Do you begin to believe that it is a lost cause, Athos?

ATHOS

I fear it; but that won't change my resolve any.

D'ARTAGNAN

And consequently mine—you know what is agreed between us, Athos— Everywhere you go I am with you—and what you do, I do—between us as in the past—so in the future and as we have the same heart we will have the same fate. But, you know, Athos, to all this there is a condition.

ATHOS

What is it?

D'ARTAGNAN

It's that if ever Monsieur Mordaunt falls between our hands—you are not to oppose what we will please to do with him.

ATHOS

D'Artagnan, why do you pursue this young man?

D'ARTAGNAN

On my honor, you are charming. Why pursue this serpent? An enraged tiger—without doubt you haven't seen him looking at King Charles in a certain way. If you had surprised that look as I have, Athos, I tell you that you would remove Mordaunt without pity or mercy. For this look says "King Charles, I will kill you as I killed the Executioner of Bethune and as I killed my uncle." When he killed de Winter, we heard him count two. Take care he doesn't count three, Athos.

PORTHOS

What's the good of bringing that up since it's a thing already decided?

ATHOS

Rumors of people. Let's see, I beg you—news of the King.

PEOPLE

Long live Parliament!

TOM LOWE

(leaving Parliament)

Condemned! Condemned!

PEOPLE

Long live Parliament!— Long live Cromwell!

D'ARTAGNAN

Come, Athos, come—all is not lost—by the devil! A Gascon always has a trick in his bag. Well—we are going to see.

ATHOS

Friend, all is finished for the King.

D'ARTAGNAN

And I tell you, it's not.

GUARDS

Move on—Move on! Stand back!

(Enter Parry)

PARRY

Sire, the name of heaven—Sire, don't look to your right as you leave.

(He tries to deflect the attention of the King who is descending the stairs from Parliament.)

KING

And why is that, my good Parry?

PARRY

Don't look I beg you—my King.

KING

But what's wrong with him then?

PARRY

Ah! What does it matter to you?

KING

Haven't you heard them reproach me with not having seen anything with my eyes. Parry, I have only thirty-six hours to live. I intend to see.

(looking past Parry)

Ah! Ah! The block—an ingenious bugbear and quite worthy of those who don't know what a gentleman is. Well, axe of the executioner, you don't frighten me—

(he strikes the block with his cane)

and I strike you—while waiting patiently and as a Christian to surrender myself to you! Come on!

(he starts walking)

So many people and not one friend.

ATHOS

Health to fallen Majesty!

PEOPLE

(in a tumult)

Ah! Ah! Death to royalists.

KING

What have I seen?

(D'Artagnan and Porthos hurl themselves to Athos' sides.)

Get back!

ARAMIS

(gliding near the King)

All is not lost yet, Sire—we are watching!

TOM LOWE

Health! Who is it said that? Wait, Majesty—here's how Tom Lowe wishes your health.

(He picks up a stone which he throws at the King—they restrain him.)

KING

The wretch—for a half crown. He'd have done it to his father.

ATHOS

Oh—the dog.

(ready to hurl himself at him)

D'ARTAGNAN

Not a word, Athos. I will deal with that man.

KING

My God! Give me resignation—sustain me in the midst of my martyrdom.

(Enter the Queen)

QUEEN

No, no—let me—I want to see him—I want to speak to him.

ATHOS

The Queen! The Queen in London!

ARAMIS

Count, a little patience!

QUEEN

Charles, my King.

(she rushes into the crowd and comes before Charles)

KING

Henriette—you here—my beloved angel— Ah, I can die now since I have seen you.

TOM LOWE

A woman. Some mistress, some courtesan. Place for Stuart's mistress.

KING

Don't deceive yourself—it's—she is neither a courtesan nor my mistress.

(He tears off her veil)

Everyone salute her, she is your Queen. You have not condemned her.

(Profound silence)

(to Queen)

Thanks, faithful and devoted heart for whom my misfortune doesn't exist, for whom sin is not an obstacle—and who like the envoys of the Lord walks over the abyss as you please. Thanks.

QUEEN

My Charles! Bless me.

KING

Oh, yes, yes! Receive the triple blessing of one who is going to die. Queen, I bless you—spouse, I bless you—mother, I bless you. Your martyrdom is sadder than mine because you will live.

QUEEN

My God! My God! Protect him!

KING

(kissing her)

Insult her now if you dare—come gentlemen, I am with you.

(The Queen follows Charles. Charles goes off—all follow him except the four friends and Tom Lowe—who remains with his companions)

ONE OF THE PEOPLE

You did wrong to insult her, Tom Lowe. It hurt me.

TOM LOWE

Ah! Because you have the heart of a coward. But it will be done again, and I will do it again.

MAN

Is it like that? Well, goodbye.

(He leaves)

TOM LOWE

(trying to pass but keeps bumping into someone)

What do you want of me?

D'ARTAGNAN

I am going to tell you.

TOM LOWE

(recoiling from d'Artagnan)

Huh?

D'ARTAGNAN

(putting his finger on Lowe's breast)

You were a coward. You insulted a defenseless man. You are going to die.

(Aramis pulls back his cape and draws his sword)

No—not with steel. Steel is for gentlemen. Porthos kill this wretch with a punch.

(Tom Lowe recoils. Porthos follows him into an alleyway. One hears a cry and the noise of a body falling.)

D'ARTAGNAN

Thus die all those who forget that a helpless man must not be touched.

ATHOS

And that a captive King is twice representative of the Lord.

PORTHOS

(coming back).

If he revives, I'll be very much surprised.

D'ARTAGNAN

Now, let each of you get ready.

ALL

For what?

D'ARTAGNAN

I have a plan.

BLACKOUT

ACT III

Scene 7

A room in Whitehall Palace—at the right, a window—at the left, a bed—at center, a large door.

(Parry sleeping in an armchair.)

KING

(stopping before Parry)

He's sleeping. His devotion has given way to fatigue. Poor old servant, who has slept by my cradle and who will sleep by my tomb. Sleep, good Parry! It seems that I am dreaming. And that what has happened to me these last fifteen days is a dream of my delirium.

(going to the window)

But, no, all is quite real. I see the muskets of the sentinels shining, I see the man working near the window. I was condemned yesterday by Parliament. I am a prisoner in Whitehall and here the portraits of my ancestors seem to keep a lively watch to see me die. Be tranquil, my noble elders—be tranquil—you will be satisfied with me.

(he sits before a table)

If I had at least one of those luminaries of the church to assist me in this supreme moment—on whose soul has sounded all the mysteries of life, all the pettiness of grandeur—perhaps his voice would stifle the voices of father and spouse that lament so in my soul. But I will have some priest of vulgar spirit who will speak to me of God and death as he would speak to other dying men—without understanding, understanding that a dying king has more things than others do to regret in this world from which he is violently torn.

(the clock strikes)

PARRY

(awakening)

Ah, My God! Pardon, pardon, sire! I slept. But in the midst of my sleep I heard the clock strike. What time is it, sir?

KING

Six o'clock. Rest assured we have still some moments to live together. It is not yet eight o'clock.

PARRY

Oh, my King, it seems to me they will not dare to commit such a sacrilege.

KING

What have they replied about my children?

PARRY

Your Majesty can see them.

KING

And for my Confessor?

PARRY

Well, since Your Majesty has chosen Mr. Juxon, Mr. Juxon receives authority to come here. Only their Puritanism was outraged to see a priest come to Your Majesty in his dress as an ecclesiastic—they demand that Mr. Juxon be dressed as a layman.

KING

And did Juxon consent?

PARRY

To accomplish the last wishes of Your Majesty, he said that he was ready for anything.

KING

Then, they are better than I hoped. Parry, I haven't slept all night and I am very fatigued.

PARRY

Sire, throw yourself on your bed. I will watch for you and I hope they will respect your sleep.

KING

Yes, an instant only to get some strength.

(He goes to bed. One hears clapping near the window.)

PARRY

Ah! My God—that was all he lacked.

KING

Parry is there a way to get the workers to make less noise?

(The noise redoubles)

PARRY

(opening the window).

Yes, sire, I am going to ask them.

SENTINEL

One cannot pass.

PARRY

Pardon—it's only to tell the workers that the King begs them to make less noise.

SENTINEL

Ah, if it's for that, speak to them.

PARRY

My friends—would you make less noise? The King is sleeping. He has need of rest.

(One sees Athos appear. Who puts his finger on his mouth)

PARRY

M. Le Comte de la Fère.

VOICE OF D'ARTAGNAN

That's fine, that's fine—tell your master that if he sleeps badly tonight he'll sleep better the next.

PARRY

(recoiling)

Great God! Am I dreaming!

(closes the window)

KING

Well?

PARRY

Sire, do you know who this worker is who made so much noise?

KING

How do you expect me to know him? Do I know this man?

PARRY

Sire, it's the Comte de la Fère.

KING

Among the workers? Are you mad, Parry?

PARRY

Yes, among the workers and who is doubtless planning to punch a hole in the wall.

KING

Huh! You've seen him?

PARRY

And Your Majesty had seen him if you had looked from the side of the window.

KING

(getting out of bed)

In fact, wasn't it he who saluted me at the moment I left Parliament?

PARRY

Yes, sire, it was he, himself.

KING

It's silly for them to say that I am a tyrant—a man who has such devoted followers. We'll be avenged by posterity.

PARRY

Sire.

KING

What?

PARRY

I hear a noise in the corridor.

KING

Who can come?

VOICE

M. Juxon!

(Aramis enters enveloped a black cloak and a wide brimmed hat.)

KING

Juxon—be welcome, Juxon. Come, Parry, don't cry any more; here God comes to us. Enter father—come, my last friend—I didn't expect they would permit me to see you.

ARAMIS

Who is this man, sire?

KING

Parry, my old servant—a devoted man and I recommended him to you after my death.

ARAMIS

Then, if it's Parry, I have nothing to fear—permit me then, sire to salute Your Majesty and to tell him on what cause I have come.

(He discovers himself)

KING

The Chevalier d'Herblay—ah how did you get here? My God—if you are recognized you will be lost.

ARAMIS

Don't think of me, think only of yourself. Your friends are watching—you see.

KING

I know it, but I cannot believe it.

ARAMIS

How do you know it?

KING

Among the workers, Parry recognized the Comte de la Fère.

ARAMIS

Fine!

KING

But how has he done it? Explain to me—is he alone.

ARAMIS

No, sire, he is with two of our friends who have joined us and are devoted to your cause.

KING

But what's done? You count on doing it?

ARAMIS

Sire, yesterday evening, at the moment when, before Your Majesty's window there stopped a carriage of carpenters, you must have heard a scream.

KING

Yes, I remember it.

ARAMIS

This scream was from the chief carpenter; a beam had fallen from the carriage and broke his leg.

KING

Well?

ARAMIS

Because of the need to proceed swiftly, he must bring four workers to the master carpenter, but because of his injury he sent one of the men with a letter of recommendation. We had purchased this letter with which we presented ourselves to the master carpenter who received us.

KING

But what is your hope?

ARAMIS

Your Majesty has said he has seen the Comte de la Fère.

KING

Yes.

ARAMIS

Well—the Comte de la Fère is piercing the wall. Under Your Majesty's window is a seeming drum with a mezzanine. The Count has penetrated this drum—lifting a plank from the parquet. As Your Majesty passes over this opening. They will reshut the plank. You will reach one of the compartments of the scaffold. A worker's clothes are prepared for you. You will descend with us—in the time that—

KING

But it will take your an enormous time to get there.

ARAMIS

The time won't fail us, sire.

KING

You forget that it is for eight o'clock.

ARAMIS

Yes, for eight o'clock. But the executioner won't be here.

KING

Where is he, then?

ARAMIS

In a cell under the hôtel Staghorn guarded by our three lackeys.

KING

In truth, you are marvelous men and if people had told me such things of you, I wouldn't have believed it. But once outside the prison, have we a way to flee?

ARAMIS

A ship that we have chartered waits for us—straight as an arrow, light as a swallow.

KING

Where is it?

ARAMIS

At Greenwich. Three nights from now, the Captain and the crew are at our disposition— We will profit by the tide, descend the Thames and in two hours we will be at sea.

KING

And who made this plan?

ARAMIS

The most adroit, the most brave, and I will say the most devoted of us four—the Chevalier D'Artagnan.

KING

A man I don't even know! Oh, My God! You don't want me to die since you make such miracles in my favor.

ARAMIS

Now, Sire, don't forget that we are watching over your health. The least sign, the least gesture, the least sign of those who approach Your Majesty—watch all, hear all, think all.

KING

Chevalier—what can I tell you? No word—comes more profoundly from my heart, nothing will ever express my recognition. If you succeed, I won't say that you saved a King. No, seen from my point of view, the crown, I swear to you is a small thing—but you will preserve a husband for his wife, a father for his children—Chevalier, touch my hand.

ARAMIS

Oh! Sire!

KING

And the Queen—what has become of her, my poor wife in the midst of this misfortune?

ARAMIS

At the moment when Your Majesty left the Parliament Square we tore the Queen away from the funereal spectacle and conducted her to our hôtel. Hardly had she learned our plans than she left us precipitously and from that moment we haven't seen her.

KING

Poor Henriette—what has become of her?

GROSLOW

(entering)

Well—it is finished, gentlemen.

KING

Why, Colonel Groslow?

GROSLOW

Because of a woman—with a pass from General Cromwell—asks to speak to you.

KING

A woman! Who could it be? Let her enter, sir.

GROSLOW

Remember you have not more than an hour.

KING

That's fine, Colonel.

GROSLOW

Enter, Madam.

(He introduces the Queen, then leaves, shutting the door.)

QUEEN

My Charles!

KING

Henriette! You, here! It's impossible, My God! Or my eyes deceive me or I am so unfortunate that I've gone mad.

QUEEN

No, my King—your eyes do not deceive you. No, Charles, you are not mad.

KING

But who let you get in to see me?

QUEEN

General Cromwell.

KING

Cromwell!

ARAMIS

Cromwell!

QUEEN

Oh, he already gave me a safe conduct to join you at the Camp but my guide got lost and we arrived too late.

KING

Cromwell! And you weren't afraid to ask a favor of this man?

QUEEN

I fear only one thing, my Charles. That's not seeing you again. Instructed in the plans of our faithful friends, I had to come to you and to get here I had only one hope: Cromwell. Be persuaded this man is not as you believe him—or at least he has impenetrable masks—immediately when you're near him your eyes are fixed on his—Your Henriette, questioned him, begged, conjured. Well, believe me, Charles, believe me Chevalier, far from applauding this terrible, public, infamous death—he abhors it. And hand on the Bible, he swore to me that he wished you health and liberty which, on account of his ambition would be more useful to him than your death. Charles, My Charles, have confidence in God, and believe that he will reunite us and that we'll never separated again and that I will accompany you in your flight, for we will find ourselves far from this bloody land, free, happy on beautiful French soil which is my country and which will become yours.

KING

What did he say to you?

QUEEN

He told me to repeat to you what he has already told you twenty times—that he was if not the most faithful servant of Your Majesty, at least he was your most loyal enemy—and the proof is he was not one of your judges.

ARAMIS

But, madam, he signed the sentence.

QUEEN

He signed it?

ARAMIS

Yes.

QUEEN

Eh! My God! Could he do otherwise in the post that he occupies and under the eyes of those who surround him?

KING

This man is an abyss. But never mind; while waiting for the smoke to clear from this abyss—you are here, Henriette—here's a friend with me—soon another.

(A knocking on the boards.)

ARAMIS

Sire, do you hear the Comte de la Fère?

KING

Is it he who knocks at my feet?

ARAMIS

It is he and you can reply to him.

(The King knocks with his cane.)

KING

What's he going to do?

ARAMIS

He's going to spend the day, thus. This evening he will open a plate of the parquet. Parry on this side will help him.

PARRY

But I have no instrument.

ARAMIS

Here's a dagger—but take care of blunting it, you may have need to dig into something besides stone.

QUEEN

Oh, the clock has struck.

KING

(listening)

Eight o'clock.

ARAMIS

You see, sire, that all is put off until tomorrow since eight o'clock is the appointed hour.

KING

Oh dear Henriette, remember well what I am going to tell you.

QUEEN

Speak, my King.

KING

Pray all your life for this gentleman you see and for the other who you hear under our feet—all your life for the other two wherever they may be who watch over my safety.

ARAMIS

Now sire, permit me to retire, our friends may have need of me—if you ask again for M. Juxon, I will return.

KING

Thanks, Chevalier—receive all expression of my recognition.

QUEEN

Chevalier, never will I forget for a single moment that I owe the life of my spouse to you and your friends. Stay.

ARAMIS

Ah! Madame—but here's the thing. I could be recognized—it's not for me that I fear but for Your Majesty. If my presence were confirmed, it would expose the plot.

QUEEN

Yes—yes. Go!

KING

Till we meet again, Chevalier.

ARAMIS

God watch over you, sire.

QUEEN

One more word, Chevalier—pardon but you understand the anguish of a spouse and a mother. This man—the executioner—is he quite seduced, bribed in our power—prisoner—he cannot flee, escape, reappear?

ARAMIS

I answer for all that, Lady.

(he goes center—one hears a step in the corridor)

QUEEN

What is that noise?

KING

One would say that it is a company of men at arms.

QUEEN

They are coming—they are getting closer.

KING

The door's opening.

(a man masked appears on the sill).

Ah, my God.

(One see the antechamber full of guards. A commissioner clerk of the Parliament enters with Groslow. He deploys on entering, his parchment.)

ARAMIS

What does this signify?

CLERK

Act of Parliament.

KING

Enough, sir—I hold the judgment read.

QUEEN

But is it really for today?

CLERK

Wasn't the King warned that it was for this morning at eight o'clock?

ARAMIS

On my soul, have they let the headsman escape?

QUEEN

(to herself)

It was only a respite of some hours, I know indeed, but a few hours would save him—I heard say—but am I then deceived? Who is this man who just appeared in the door—terrible under his black mask.

GROSLOW

The Executioner of London has vanished—but in his place a man volunteered. There won't be any delay then in the time asked by Charles Stuart to put his temporal affairs in order—for the others will be finished.

ARAMIS

Ah. My God!

KING

(embracing him)

Courage!

(to Colonel)

Sir, I am ready—I desire only one thing—to embrace my children who for three years I have not seen and whom I will not see again except in heaven.

GROSLOW

They've been waiting for a quarter of an hour.

QUEEN

(falling on her knees)

Oh, my God!

ARAMIS

Where is God, sire—what is God doing?

KING

Don't desolate yourself thus, my child! You ask: where is God? You don't see him because earthly possessions hide him. You ask me what he's doing? He's watching your devotion and my martyrdom and believe me, both will have their reward—take then what comes to you from men and not from God—these are the men who make me die—these are the men who make you cry!

QUEEN

(swaying)

Have pity! Have pity! Have pity!

KING

Henriette, don't break my strength with your tears which tear my heart—you are not the wife of Charles Stuart—you are the Queen of England.

(They bring in the King's children.)

QUEEN

My Children!

KING

My son, you've seen many people in the streets and halls of this palace—you will see those who surround you again. These people are going to kill your father. Don't tell me that you will never forget it. For they perhaps will call on you one day to wear the crown which at this moment they tear from my head. Don't accept it, my son, if you must return to this palace escorted by hatred and rage—be then good, clement, forgetful and avert your eyes when you believe you see my shadow pass under these arches—for if you have a reign of vengeance and reprisal, you won't be able, even in your bed, to die without fear and remorse—as I am going to die—on a scaffold! And now your hand in mine—swear, my child—

(the child bursts into tears hiding his head in his father's breast)

And you my daughter

(he takes the young Henriette in his arms)

You, my child—never forget me!

(the young princess embraces her father who takes her hand and places it on the arm of the Queen)

Now, Henriette, our children have no one except their mother. Goodbye.

QUEEN

Oh, live, and live here, in my arms, here in my heart—and in a moment—no, no gentlemen, it is impossible—for now, this man is your king who is all powerful—- he who holds the life of a people in his hand—one cannot kill him—his life is inviolable, sacred. My God, he is your image on earth—My God, I call to you! It is my Charles, my spouse—he is the father of my children—my children, pray my children—on your knees.

(the children kneel)

(The Queen wants to go to her knees but lacks the strength)

Oh, help—I am dying)

(she falls to her knees, arms extended and faints letting out a scream)

KING

Parry, I confide the Queen to you

(to Aramis)

Chevalier, a last service—your arm—Gentlemen, I am with you— let's march!

(The Cortege reforms—one hears the cheers—the Great Clock of Westminster—the King leaves by the left)

BLACKOUT

ACT III

Scene 8

The window of Whitehall. The scaffold draped in black leans against the window. At the rise of the Curtain, Athos is seated under the scaffold drapes which hide him from the people—digs a tunnel under the window.

ATHOS

(striking the wall)

In a few minutes the secret passage will be completely open—D'Artagnan and Porthos ought to be at their posts on the square—as for Aramis, he can penetrate even to the King and instruct him in our plans. But how comes it that I don't hear the agreed signal? Once only they struck on the flagstone of the chimney and I responded—but for a quarter of an hour, no noise, no warnings are coming to me. This silence is frightening. The immobility freezes my heart. These bloody spectators are waiting. Yes, keep your eyes on the window—in a few moments, and the signal is going to come to my ear and I will run off with your prey—but there's a noise of arms it seems to me.

(he opens the tapestry with his dagger)

What did I see? Cavaliers, halberds and below the first ranks of the people who look like a somber ocean—foaming and roaring. My God, what has happened? Among the spectators who all have their eyes fixed on the window—I don't perceive D'Artagnan, who's he looking at? Ah—what is that noise? Who is tramping on this funereal road?

(The Halberdiers appear on the scaffold.)

PEOPLE

(outside)

The Executioner! The Executioner!

ATHOS

The Executioner—is it true in the end?

(The King advances, followed by Aramis)

KING

(to Groslow)

A moment, I pray you.

ATHOS

That voice! It's the King.

(wiping his face)

But why has he left the palace?

KING

(looking around him)

No one! All is then finished for me!

(to the people who cannot be seen)

You English—and all you who are the authors and accomplices of my murder—I pardon you. Without doubt during the course of my life, short as it has been, I have committed some injustices. Kings cannot be exempt from error—and those who have suffered come to see me die. So let them pardon me in their turn.

(the colonel approaches)

Wait—I haven't finished.

ATHOS

Oh! Nothing, nothing can save him!

KING

(continuing)

People—one day you will understand my conduct, one day you will do justice to my memory. While waiting, satisfy like the sea your fury and your blind resentment. That is just since heaven permits it.

ATHOS

Mon Dieu! Mon Dieu!

(King, taking from his breast a cross of diamonds and giving it to Aramis)

KING

Sir, I will keep this cross just to the last moment—you will take it when I am dead.

ARAMIS

Yes, sire, you will be obeyed.

ATHOS

The voice of Aramis! At least he has a friend with him.

KING

(to the Executioner)

Now, you, listen, I don't want death to surprise me. I will kneel to pray—let them wait till I open my arms saying "Remember," then...

(to Assistants)

Here's the moment to leave the world, gentlemen; I leave you in the midst of the storm and proceed you to that unknown country. Good-bye.

(he looks at Aramis and nods to him)

Now separate yourself and let me make my prayer freely.

(he kneels as if he wished to kiss the platform)

Comte de la Fère, are you there, and can I speak?

ATHOS

(trembling)

Yes, Majesty.

KING

Faithful friend, generous heart, I cannot be saved by you. I ought not to be. Now, even though I commit a sacrilege, I will speak to you.— yes, I have spoken to men. I have spoken to God. You will be the last I speak to. To sustain a cause I believed sacred, I have lost the throne of my fathers and divested the inheritance of my children— you love them, right—Comte de la Fère?

ATHOS

Oh Majesty!

KING

I confide to you, my last friend, I confide to you the care of bringing my last farewell to my Queen—Let her hope! Let her live for our children. Count, here's my last wish—you hear me?

ATHOS

Yes, Majesty.

KING

You will speak often of me to my son— You will tell him I bless him and I love him. You also, I love you, and I bless you—thank your noble friends and for what you have done for me on earth, I am going to pray God to render you in heaven—where we will meet— Now, Comte de la Fère, bid me adieu.

ATHOS

(babbling, freezing with terror)

Adieu, Majesty—saint and martyr.

(The King rises and leaves, supported by Aramis.)

ATHOS

They walk. They separate. Oh, My God! My God! You won't speak to me again, Sire!

(He listens at the left and leaves for a moment.)

KING

Remember!

A VOICE

Three.

(Athos returns to the scene, tottering.)

ATHOS

Dead! The King dead! Oh!

(He falls in a faint.)

CURTAIN

ACT IV

Scene 9

An isolated house at the Port of London. At right an avenue of trees bordering on the house. At left—the wall of the screened cloister. At center—city gate—Westminster in the horizon. It is snowing.

(A man wrapped in a black cloak, with a large hat pulled down over a mask—leaves the city gate and advances cautiously towards the door of the isolated house. One distinguishes under his mask a graying beard. He looks with care around him and decides to open the door of the house then he looks around, and enters swiftly. Hardly has the door shut then D'Artagnan appears at the angle of the City Gate and advances rapidly on the track of the unknown who he has seen enter.)

D'ARTAGNAN

(looking at the house)

He is there.

(he makes a sign to Grimaud, Mousqueton, and Blaisois, who follow in his footsteps)

Blaisois—you remember the route we've just taken. Run to the hôtel, bring the Gentlemen here—and not a word of explanation—only that I expect them. Run quickly.

(he goes toward the house)

A door at the rear—are there any other exits?

(he makes a turn around the house)

GRIMAUD

(regarding the sky)

Black!

MOUSQUETON

Brrr! How cold!

D'ARTAGNAN

(returning)

Another door giving on this empty quay. Grimaud—near that door you will find a pillar. Hide you behind it.

(speaking into his ear)

GRIMAUD

(opens his cloak and shows a large cutlass)

Yes.

(Grimaud leaves)

D'ARTAGNAN

Mousqueton from this corner you can see everything, hear everything. Let anyone go in, but if someone leaves, call. I am going to glance at the surroundings of the place— Apropos.

(he speaks in his ear. Mousqueton opens his cloak and displays two pistols)

Fine!

(Mousqueton places himself at the corner of the house, head projecting, in a way to watch the door. D'Artagnan goes out right.)

ATHOS

(entering)

But what way are we going to take?

BLAISOIS

The best way, gentlemen.

ARAMIS

Beaten by fate!

ATHOS

Noble and unfortunate King! God has abandoned us.

PORTHOS

Don't be desolated, Count, we are all mortal— But why the devil didn't D'Artagnan return? Why did he send us Blaisois? Why didn't Blaisois say anything when he came? Has something happened to D'Artagnan?

ARAMIS

We are going to learn, since he sent for us.

PORTHOS

I lost him in the alley.

ATHOS

Oh, I've seen him. He was in the first row of the crowd admirably placed so as to lose nothing, and all in all, the spectacle was curious. He would have wished to see it out.

D'ARTAGNAN

(who on the last words of Athos enters from the right)

Ah, Comte de le Fère—it is you who are slandering those who are not present.

ALL

D'Artagnan.

PORTHOS

Now, there he is!

I don't slander you, my friend, we are uneasy about you and I was telling where I had seen you—you didn't know King Charles. He was only a stranger to you—you weren't forced to love him.

(in saying these words, he holds his hand to D'Artagnan. D'Artagnan pretends not to see the gesture and keeps his hand under his cloak.)

PORTHOS

Come on, since we are reunited, let's leave.

ATHOS

Yes, let's leave this abominable country. The boat is waiting for us. You know it. Let's leave this evening. We have nothing more to do in England.

D'ARTAGNAN

You are indeed rushed, Count.

ATHOS

This bloody soil burns my feet.

D'ARTAGNAN

Snow doesn't do that to me.

ATHOS

But what do you want us to do here now the King is dead?

D'ARTAGNAN

(negligently)

You don't see there remains something for you to do in England.

ATHOS

Nothing—nothing except to doubt divine goodness and to scorn my own strength.

D'ARTAGNAN

Well, weak, bloody idler that I am, who placed myself thirty feet from the scaffold to better see fall the head of a King, I didn't know and who—at least he so appears—was indifferent to me—I think differently than the Count! I am staying.

PORTHOS

Ah, you're staying in London?

D'ARTAGNAN

Yes—And you?

PORTHOS

(embarrassed)

Damnation! If you stay—as I came with you. I cannot go without you. I cannot leave you alone in this frightful country.

D'ARTAGNAN

Thanks, my excellent friend. Then I have a little business to propose to you and which we will put into execution if Monsieur le Comte will play a role. The idea of came to me while I was watching the spectacle you know about.

PORTHOS

Which is?

D'ARTAGNAN

To know who this masked man is who volunteered so obligingly to cut off the head of the King.

ATHOS

A masked man—you didn't let the Executioner escape?

D'ARTAGNAN

The Executioner, he's still locked in the hall below our hôtel.

ATHOS

Who is the wretch who laid a hand on our King?

ARAMIS

An amateur Executioner who not withstanding wields an axe with facility—for it only took one blow.

PORTHOS

I am angry not to have followed him.

D'ARTAGNAN

Well, my dear Porthos, that was exactly the idea which came to me.

ATHOS

Pardon me, D'Artagnan. I doubted God—I could even doubt you—pardon me.

D'ARTAGNAN

We will see all this in an hour.

ARAMIS

Well—

D'ARTAGNAN

While I watched, not the King as the Count thought—for I knew he was a man who was going to die, and although I've become accustomed to this sort of thing, it always makes me ill. But rather, the masked Executioner. The idea came to me, thus as I told you, to know who he was. Since, we aid each other and calling each other's help like a second hand to the aid of the first, I looked around me to see if Porthos was there—for I had seen you near the King, Aramis. And you Count, I knew you were under the scaffold—which made me pardon you, for I knew you were suffering. I saw in the crowd Grimaud, Mousqueton, and Blaisois. I signaled them not to go. Everything over—you know in what lugubrious fashion—the people left, little by little. Evening came, I had retired to a corner of the square with my men and I looked for the Executioner who went into the Royal Chamber, enveloped in his cloak and disappeared. I divined he was going to leave and ran to the door. In fact, five minutes later we saw him descend the stair.

ATHOS

You followed him?

D'ARTAGNAN

By God! But not without trouble. Now after a half hour's march across the most torturous streets in the city, he came to a little isolated house where not a noise, not a light announced the presence of anyone—without doubt the one we pursue believes himself alone—for I heard the grating of a key, a door opened and he disappeared.

ATHOS

But this house?

ALL

This house.

D'ARTAGNAN

(pointing)

Right here.

ALL

Oh!

(They want to rush in.)

D'ARTAGNAN

(stopping them)

Wait.

(he strikes his hands—Mousqueton rises)

Nobody left the house, I hope?

MOUSQUETON

No, sire.

D'ARTAGNAN

Someone has come in?

MOUSQUETON

No, sir.

D'ARTAGNAN

And by the other door—

MOUSQUETON

I don't know—it's Grimaud who's watching the door.

D'ARTAGNAN

Go relieve him, and have him come here.

(Mousqueton leaves; Grimaud enters after a moment.)

GRIMAUD

(entering)

Here I am.

D'ARTAGNAN

Nobody entered by the door you guarded?

GRIMAUD

No.

D'ARTAGNAN

No one left?

GRIMAUD

No.

D'ARTAGNAN

Then all is as when I left you?

GRIMAUD

Yes.

D'ARTAGNAN

He is in this room.

PORTHOS

Effectively—one sees the light.

ARAMIS

You must be able to see from the balcony.

D'ARTAGNAN

Porthos, my friend, place yourself there—and if it doesn't humiliate you to serve as a step to Grimaud.

PORTHOS

What then?

(Grimaud mounts on his shoulders to reach the balcony)

D'ARTAGNAN

Well?

ATHOS

Can you see?

GRIMAUD

I see.

D'ARTAGNAN

What?

GRIMAUD

Two men.

D'ARTAGNAN

Do you know them?

GRIMAUD

Wait.

D'ARTAGNAN

Who are they?

GRIMAUD

One is writing.

ATHOS

Who is it?

GRIMAUD

I believe it's....

D'ARTAGNAN

Well?

GRIMAUD

Wait.

D'ARTAGNAN

Let's see.

GRIMAUD

General Oliver Cromwell.

ATHOS, PORTHOS & ARAMIS

What does he say?

D'ARTAGNAN

I suspected it! But the other one we followed.

GRIMAUD

He is in the shadow—he's approaching the general.

(He utters a cry and jumps from Porthos' shoulders.)

PORTHOS

Well, what then?

D'ARTAGNAN

You have seen him. Speak quickly.

GRIMAUD

Mordaunt.

(The three friends utter a cry of joy.)

ATHOS

(aside)

Fatality.

D'ARTAGNAN

A moment, gentlemen, this is becoming interesting. Go my brave Grimaud. Remount your observatory, the least gesture will betray us to these men. You at the door, Aramis—you with me, Porthos; you, Athos: Watch!

BLACKOUT

ACT IV

Scene 10

The interior of the house of Cromwell—chamber shut by a door on the right. One sees the window which gives on the balcony from the same side.

MORDAUNT

Your Honor gave me these two Frenchmen when they were only guilty of taking arms in favor of Charles. Now they are guilty of plotting against England. Your honor intends to give me all four of them?

CROMWELL

Take them.

(Mordaunt bows with a smile of triumphant ferocity).

But let's return, if you please, to this unfortunate Charles. Did they cry among the people?

MORDAUNT

Very little—but only "Long Live Cromwell".

CROMWELL

Where were you placed?

MORDAUNT

I was where I could see and hear everything.

CROMWELL

It appears that the masked man fulfilled his office well.

MORDAUNT

(in a calm voice).

In fact, a single blow of the axe.

CROMWELL

Perhaps he was a man of that trade.

MORDAUNT

Do you think so, sir?

CROMWELL

Why not?

MORDAUNT

The man didn't have the manner of an executioner.

CROMWELL

And who but an executioner would do this frightful job?

MORDAUNT

Perhaps some personal enemy of King Charles who had made a vow of vengeance and who accomplished this vow; perhaps some gentleman who had grave reasons for hating the fallen King and who knowing he was going to flee and escape him, placed himself in his way, face masked, and hatchet in hand—not as a replacement for the Executioner but as a proxy of fate.

CROMWELL

It's possible.

MORDAUNT

And if he was so, Your Honor would condemn his action?

CROMWELL

It's not for me to judge—it's an affair between him and God.

MORDAUNT

But if Your Honor knew this gentleman?

CROMWELL

I don't know him, sir, and I don't wish to know him. What does it matter to me that it was this one or another one? From the moment Charles was condemned, it wasn't a man that cut off his head but an axe.

MORDAUNT

And yet, without the man the King was saved. You said it yourself. They would have run off with him.

CROMWELL

Only to Greenwich. There they would have embarked on a boat rented yesterday by his saviors. But on this boat, in place of Captain Crabbe whom they expected, are four men of mine and four tons of the nation's powder. At sea the four men would escape in a small boat which followed the boat, abandoning the King and his saviors in the boat. You are too well instructed for me to have to explain the rest.

MORDAUNT

Yes, they'd all jump in the sea.

CROMWELL

Exactly. The explosion would do what the axe had not. King Charles would disappear, annihilated. They would say that he escaped human justice, he was still pursued and killed by celestial vengeance—we weren't his judges it was heaven which struck him.

MORDAUNT

Sir, as always I bow and humble myself before you—you are a profound thinker and your idea of mining the boat is sublime.

CROMWELL

Absurd since it has become useless. There is no sublime idea except one which bears fruits. All ideas that abort are foolish and arid. You will go then to Greenwich this evening, Mordaunt, you will ask the Captain of the ship *Éclair* to show you a white handkerchief knotted at four ends. It was the sign agreed between the Frenchmen and Captain Crabbe—you will tell my men to come ashore and you will deliver the powder to the arsenal.

MORDAUNT

At least this ship, such as it is, cannot serve projects useful to the nation.

CROMWELL

I understand.

MORDAUNT

Ah milord! Milord! God in making you His Elect has given you his look which none can escape.

CROMWELL

I know you call me, "milord," and that's fine when we are alone—but we must pay attention that such a word not escape you before the Puritans.

MORDAUNT

Isn't your honor going to be called so soon?

CROMWELL

(rising and taking his cloak)

I hope to be, at least, but it is not yet time.

MORDAUNT

You are going, sir.

CROMWELL

Yes, I slept here yesterday and the day before, and you know it is not my custom to sleep three nights in the same bed.

MORDAUNT

Then, Your Honor, gives me liberty for the night?

CROMWELL

And even for the entire day tomorrow if need be— Will you come with me, Mordaunt?

MORDAUNT

Thanks, sir—the detours you are obliged to take in passing through the underworld waste my time. And after all, you have told me I have perhaps lost too much. I will go by the other door.

CROMWELL

(pushing on a button hidden by the tapestry, leaves by a secret door.)

In that case, adieu.

(At the moment that Cromwell disappears by a secret door— Grimaud appears on the balcony. Mordaunt has put on his cape. He takes the lamp on the table and leaves. The window is open. Porthos and Aramis come into the room. Soon after, Mordaunt returns, pale, appalling, recoiling, lamp in hand, before D'Artagnan who, hat low, walks towards him with an exquisite politeness. Behind D'Artagnan, Athos.)

D'ARTAGNAN

Monsieur Mordaunt, since after so many days lost in running after each other—chance brings us together—let's chat a little, if you please.

MORDAUNT

I hear you, sir.

D'ARTAGNAN

It seems to me, sir, that you change costume as rapidly as I have seen Italian mimes do that Cardinal Mazarin brought from Bergamo. No doubt you saw them during your stay in France.

ARAMIS

Before you were disguised, I mean to say dressed, as an assassin—and now—

MORDAUNT

And now, to the contrary, I seem to be in the dress of one who is going to be assassinated, right?

PORTHOS

Ah, sir, how can you say such things when you are in the company of gentlemen and when you have such a good sword at your side?

MORDAUNT

It isn't such a good sword, sir, which faces four swords, without counting the swords and daggers of your acolytes who wait you at the door.

ARAMIS

Pardon, sir. You are in error. Those who wait at the door are not acolytes, they are our lackeys. I intend to establish things in their most scrupulous verity.

D'ARTAGNAN

But that is not the question. And I return to my question. I gave my-self the honor of asking you, sir, why you change your exterior? The mask was good enough for you, it seemed to me—the grey beard became your marvelously and the axe with which you furnished us so illustrious a blow— Couldn't go better with you at this time. Why then have you changed?

MORDAUNT

Because in recalling the scene in Armentiers, I thought I would find four axes for one since I was looking for four executioners.

D'ARTAGNAN

(calmly)

Sir, although profoundly vicious and corrupt, you are young—which makes me halt this frivolous discussion with you—yes, frivolous, for what you have just said of Armentiers has not the least to do with the situation presented here. In fact, we couldn't offer a sword to madame, your mother—and pray her to fence against us. But you, sir, as a young Cavalier who plays with dagger, pistol and axe as we have seen you do, and who has at his side, a sword of such a cut as this has the right to ask the favor of a meeting.

MORDAUNT

Ah! Ah! Then it's a duel that you wish?

D'ARTAGNAN

(with cold blood)

Pardon, pardon, but we are in a rush—for each of us must prefer that things happen according to the rules—sit down again, dear Porthos, and you, Monsieur Mordaunt, try to remain calm. We are going to regulate this affair as best we can, and I am going to be frank with you. Admit, Monsieur Mordaunt that you very much desire to kill us all.

MORDAUNT

All.

D'ARTAGNAN

(turning to Aramis)

It's a great joy, you will agree, Aramis, that M. Mordaunt under-stands us so well. At least there will be no misunderstanding be-tween us.

(turning back to Mordaunt)

Dear Mr. Mordaunt, I say to you that these gentlemen, in their turn, return your kind sentiments and will be delighted to kill you, too. I will say more—it is they who will kill you in all probability. To-gether they are loyal gentlemen and the best proof I can furnish is here.

(In saying these words he throws his hat to the floor, pushes his chair against the wall and makes sign to his friends to do the same, then bowing to Mordaunt graciously.)

At your orders, sir—for if you have nothing to say against the honor I claim it is I who will begin, if you please.

PORTHOS

Stop—I will begin—and without rhetoric.

ARAMIS

Permit me, Porthos.

D'ARTAGNAN

Gentlemen, gentlemen, be easy. You will have your turn. Stay in your place, like Athos to whose calm I recommend you and leave to me the initiative I have taken.

(Drawing his sword with a terrible gesture)

Besides, I have a particular affair with monsieur and I will begin, I want it. I intend to have it.

(to Mordaunt)

Sir, I am waiting for you.

MORDAUNT

And I, gentlemen, I admire you! You dispute who will begin to fight against me and you don't consult me about it. And this business concerns me too—it seems to me—I hate you all, true—but to different degrees. I hope to kill you all—but I have the best chance of killing the first more than second, the second more than the third and the third more than the last. I claim the right to choose my adversary—if you deny me this right—kill me—I will not fight.

PORTHOS & ARAMIS

It is just, he is right.

MORDAUNT

Well, I choose for my first adversary whichever of you—not being worthy of the name the Count de la Fère—is called Athos.

ATHOS

(shaking his head)

Mr. Mordaunt, any duel between us is impossible—give someone else the honor you destine to me.

MORDAUNT

Ah—there's already one of you who's afraid.

D'ARTAGNAN

Double Damnation!

(jumping)

Who said that Athos was afraid?

ATHOS

(with a smile of sadness and scorn)

Let me speak, D'Artagnan.

D'ARTAGNAN

This is your decision, Athos?

ATHOS

Irrevocable.

D'ARTAGNAN

Fine, let's not speak any more about it.

(to Mordaunt)

You have heard sir. The Comte de la Fère doesn't wish to have the honor of fighting with you. Choose among us which one will replace him.

MORDAUNT

Since I cannot fight with him, it doesn't matter to me with whom I fight. Put your names in a hat and I will draw by chance.

D'ARTAGNAN

There's an idea.

ARAMIS

In fact, this way's agreeable to all.

PORTHOS

I hadn't thought of—now it's very simple.

D'ARTAGNAN

Let's see Aramis, write with the pretty little script you wrote to Marie Michon to warn her that the mother of this gentlemen wished to assassinate milord Buckingham.

(Aramis goes to Cromwell's bureau, tears three sheets off equal size, writes a name on each, then presents them to Mordaunt—who without reading them signals that he is in perfect agreement. Aramis roles the papers, puts them in a hat and presents them to Mordaunt who draws one and lets the others fall with disdain.)

Ah, young serpent, I will sacrifice all my chance of promotion to Captain for that paper to carry my name.

ARAMIS

(reading the paper in a loud voice)

D'Artagnan.

D'ARTAGNAN

Ah, there's still justice in heaven.

(returning toward Mordaunt)

I hope, sire, that you have no objection to doing it?

MORDAUNT

(drawing his sword and leaning on the point)

None, sir.

D'ARTAGNAN

Are you ready, sir?

MORDAUNT

I am waiting for you, sir.

D'ARTAGNAN

Then take care of yourself, sir, I draw my sword often enough.

MORDAUNT

And I, too.

D'ARTAGNAN

So much the better! That puts my conscience at ease. En garde!

MORDAUNT

One moment. Give your word gentlemen, that you won't charge me all at once.

PORTHOS

Is it to have the pleasure of insulting us that you ask us this, sir?

MORDAUNT

No—it's to have, as the gentleman just said, an easy conscience.

D'ARTAGNAN

(looking around him)

It must be for something else.

PORTHOS & ARAMIS

Word of a gentleman.

MORDAUNT

In that case, gentlemen, place yourselves in some corner as the Comte de la Fère has done, who doesn't wish to fight me but appears at least to know the rules of combat. And leave us space, we are going to need it.

ARAMIS

So be it.

PORTHOS

There's a lot of fuss.

D'ARTAGNAN

Arrange yourselves, gentlemen, there's no need to give the gentleman the least pretext for bad conduct. Come on, are you ready, sir?

MORDAUNT

I am.

(They cross swords.)

D'ARTAGNAN

Ah, you break away, you turn! As you like it—I will gain something—I won't see your nasty face—here I am now in the shadows. So much the better. You don't have any idea what a false look you have sir, when you are afraid. Look at my eyes and you will see a thing your mirror never shows you ever—that is to say a loyal and frank face.

(Mordaunt jumping back finds himself near wall on which he leans with his left hand).

Ah—now this time, don't break away anymore, my fine friend. Gentlemen, have you ever seen a scorpion cling to a wall?

(At the moment when more relentless than ever, after a rapid and close feint, he hurls himself like lightening on Mordaunt, the wall seems to split. Mordaunt disappears through the gaping opening and the sword pressed between two panels breaks. D'Artagnan takes a step back. The wall shuts.)

Help, Gentlemen! Let's break this door.

ARAMIS

(running towards D'Artagnan.)

He's the demon incarnate.

PORTHOS

(pressing his shoulder against the secret door)

He's escaping us, by God, he's escaping us!

ATHOS

(sourly)

So much the better!

D'ARTAGNAN

I thought as much, by God! I thought as much—when the wretch turned around the room I foresaw some infamous maneuver. I knew that he contrived something but who could suspect this?

ARAMIS

It's a frightful misfortune that the devil, his friend, sends us.

ATHOS

It's a great good fortune, God sends us.

D'ARTAGNAN

In truth, you surrender, Athos! How can you say such things to people like us! God's blood! You don't understand the situation? The wretch is going to send us a hundred ironsides. Who will grind us like grain in the mortar of Mr. Cromwell— Come on, come on, en route! If we remain even five minutes here, it's all over with us.

ATHOS & ARAMIS

Yes, you are right. En route.

PORTHOS

And where are we going?

D'ARTAGNAN

To the hôtel, take our clothes and our horses. Then from there, if it please, God, to France, where at least I know the architecture of the houses. Our ship is waiting for us—my word it's still lucky—en route.

ALL

En route! En route!

BLACKOUT

ACT V

Scene 11

The *Lightning* at anchor. One can see the bridge of the poop deck chamber with a large window cut away—giving on the sea. Outside the poop deck chamber, a compartment filled with gross tonnage on top of each other—the foremost real, the background painted. A little stairway leads from this compartment to the bridge. On the left, on the bridge another compartment with two doors, the one at the right opening on the magazine—the other to the left, hammocks, a suspended table. It's night.

SENTINEL

(on the bridge)

Hey! From the bank—halt there! Who goes there?

(Groslow on the bridge. He is enveloped in a fisherman's cloak—beard cut)

VOICE

Officer—from General Cromwell.

GROSLOW

Advance slowly! Mr. Mordaunt! What is it? Is anything amiss?

MORDAUNT

(on the bridge—looking at him attentively)

You, colonel? Ah, very good. Everything's ship-shape on the contrary. But is there nothing new on the *Lightning*? Has nothing changed recently?

GROSLOW

Nothing—but while you are here—what has happened down there?

MORDAUNT

All has happened as it must be expected.

GROSLOW

Then....

MORDAUNT

(showing the knotted handkerchief)

Then you see I know everything.

GROSLOW

That's true.

MORDAUNT

Let's not lose time, for they'll soon be here.

GROSLOW

Who?

MORDAUNT

The four conspirators who wanted to rescue the King and did not succeed.

GROSLOW

Ah—it's them that Mr. Cromwell desires—? Fine—I understand.

They are coming, you say?

MORDAUNT

Yes—so rapidly, so furiously, that on my way I always heard a galloping of their horses behind me—they are coming, I tell you! But—they know you—they will suspect you.

GROSLOW

Impossible. Under this cloak in the night—and then you see—in accordance with the general's order, I have cut my beard and I will disguise my voice.

MORDAUNT

Yes, it's true! I myself hardly recognized you. You will lodge them.

GROSLOW

In the cabin on the poop deck just under the cargo of wine.

MORDAUNT

Yes, but their servants?

GROSLOW

Their servants in the bridge hold—with door quite bolted.

MORDAUNT

And I—for if they see me, all will be lost.

GROSLOW

In my cabin, behind a false closet which seems to be the wall of a ship—there's an impenetrable hiding place even for customs agents looking for contraband. I will answer for you. Besides you will see.

MORDAUNT

(eyes fixed on the sea)

There's a bark approaching—oh—now.

GROSLOW

What sight you have.

MORDAUNT

(always watching)

I have the sight of a man whose life depends on his vision. I tell you, it is a bark directing itself toward the ship.

GROSLOW

In fact, I see it now. Sentinel, on guard and remember the password.

SENTINEL

Yes, commander.

MORDAUNT

They are here—all! Quite all of them!

GROSLOW

Come on—hide—then when they are installed.... Come.

SENTINEL

Hey—from the bark—Ho there! Who goes there?

D'ARTAGNAN'S VOICE

Louis and France.

GROSLOW

(returning)

Let them come on board. Come on board, gentlemen, I've been waiting for you.

D'ARTAGNAN

(stopping Athos)

That's not the voice of Captain Crabbe. It's not his shape—it's not him. A moment, Athos.

ATHOS

Who are you, friend? And why do you say you were waiting for us? No one knows you.

GROSLOW

I know, milord. You were looking for Captain Crabbe—but you cannot see him.

D'ARTAGNAN

Excuse me! Why can't we see him?

GROSLOW

Alas, milord, my poor brother-in-law, Captain Crabbe, fell from the top mast this morning and has already broken his leg.

D'ARTAGNAN

(suspicious)

That's an unlucky accident. Stay on your guard, Athos.

GROSLOW

But Milord, this white handkerchief knotted at the four ends that your companion holds in his hand—and one which similarly knotted is in my pocket will prove to you.

D'ARTAGNAN

That's all right.

(to Groslow)

But there's something else.

GROSLOW

Yes, milord—you promised to Captain Crabbe, my brother-in-law—seventy-five pounds if you arrive safe and sound in Boulogne or at some other port on the coast of France of your choice.

ATHOS

(to D'Artagnan)

Well, what do you say to that?

D'ARTAGNAN

I say that....

(he clicks his tongue as a sign of scorn)

ATHOS

We haven't the time to be suspicious.

D'ARTAGNAN

At least, we can be on our guard even in entering this ship we will watch this man—and if he doesn't behave properly, he'd better watch out!

ATHOS

I am going to call our rear guard—Grimaud, tell these gentlemen to go aboard and send back the bark on which we came.

GROSLOW

Your lordships will stay on board?

ATHOS

Yes.

D'ARTAGNAN

A moment! How many men have you here?

GROSLOW

Ten, milord, without counting myself.

D'ARTAGNAN

Ten. Oh! I'm relieved—but tell me where will you put us?

GROSLOW

Here milord—in the cabin on the poop.

ATHOS

And our servants?

GROSLOW

In the hold, milord—André—install them.

ANDRÉ

Come, gentlemen.

D'ARTAGNAN

Very good! What's your name?

GROSLOW

Rogers, milord—this way!

(he points the lackeys to the stairs to the hold. Mousqueton goes down, then Blaisois, Grimaud the last)

D'ARTAGNAN

You, my friends, try to get a good as possible lodging—while I am going to make a tour of the ship.

ATHOS

Take Grimaud with you.

D'ARTAGNAN

To do what?

ATHOS

One doesn't know what may happen—take Grimaud.

PORTHOS

And find out, by the way, if there's something for supper.

D'ARTAGNAN

Grimaud—take this lantern—follow me, Captain Rogers. Ten minutes, my friend, and I return.

(they go down)

MOUSQUETON

(in the hold)

How low it is here. How cold we will be tonight! How hard it will be for us to sleep—if, by chance a storm at sea—right, Blaisois?

BLAISOIS

I am familiar with the inconveniences of this element.

D'ARTAGNAN

(descending under the powder kegs, a pistol behind his back)

Where are we here?

GROSLOW

(on the ladder)

You see, milord—it's a magazine.

D'ARTAGNAN

How many kegs! You could call this the Cavern of Ali Baba— What's down here, then?

(taking the lantern from the hands of Grimaud and looking about)

GROSLOW

(quickly turning)

Port wine, milord.

D'ARTAGNAN

Ah! Port wine. That's always a luxury—then our Porthos will be sure at least of not dying of thirst. And these kegs are full.

(he brings his lantern closer)

GROSLOW

(nervous)

Some others are empty.

(D'Artagnan taps his fingers on the kegs and inserts his lantern into the intervals of the casks)

D'ARTAGNAN

Everything's fine. I'll answer for this compartment. Let's go on, Mr. Rogers.

(They go into the cabin.)

ARAMIS

(in the cabin on the poop)

Well, Porthos—what do you say of England?

PORTHOS

It's nice to go there—but it's wonderful to leave.

ATHOS

Alas, we are returning alone.

ARAMIS

Let's sleep.

PORTHOS

Ah, so—but you're not hungry?

D'ARTAGNAN

Ah—here's where our men are lodged.

(he looks over the whole compartment).

You must sleep, my brave ones. Grimaud, I don't need you any-more. Thanks.

(aside)

Nothing here, either.

(to Groslow)

Captain, where does this door go?

GROSLOW

Pardon milord, I have the key—it's my cabin.

D'ARTAGNAN

Let's see—and thus show me the main hold.

GROSLOW

Enter—milord, you go up to your room by the stair from my cabin which leads to the bridge.

MOUSQUETON

(watching D'Artagnan leave)

There's an officer who knows how to make his rounds!

BLAISOIS

With masters like these, one can enjoy the softness of sleep.

ATHOS

D'Artagnan is not yet back.

ARAMIS

In fact, I hear his voice—he's making a tour of the ship and here he is leaving the hatch down there.

D'ARTAGNAN

(reappearing on the bridge with his lantern)

The main hold is empty—nothing suspect in the Captain's quarters, if there was any army abroad, it could only be an army of rats. Well Captain Rogers, here I am in the cabin on the poop—begin, watch all maneuvers and try to get us there quickly.

GROSLOW

(from a distance)

Yes, milord.

PORTHOS

What news?

D'ARTAGNAN

Excellent, we can sleep with the same peace of mind as when we are lodged in the Chevrette, rue Tiquetonne.

(Drawing his sword from its scabbard, checking his pistol and sitting down behind the door)

ATHOS

Well, what are you doing then? You call this peace of mind? You still fear something then?

D'ARTAGNAN

The best way to be truly secure is to always be fearful of not being so—come on, my friends, take strength—I see quite well what afflicts you Athos but you have often said it—we can blame fate. Aramis, you are going to see your duchesses again—have beautiful dreams—you dear Porthos, I know well what you lack—but I promise tomorrow at Boulogne, some oysters, Spanish wine, and an Amiens pâté—for tomorrow noon we will be in France.

ATHOS

The country of loyal hearts.

ARAMIS

And living women.

PORTHOS

Burgundy wine.

ALL

Till tomorrow, in France—Goodnight, friends!

(They shake hands and sleep)

GRIMAUD

(making a calculation in the depth of the cabin)

Twenty-three Louis.

BLAISOIS

What's he say.

MOUSQUETON

In his quality of treasurer, he keeps the daily accounts of the society, but don't make me talk Blaisois.

BLAISOIS

You must eat and drink, that will restore you.

GRIMAUD

(still calculating)

Forty-one, forty-two….

MOUSQUETON

Eat barley bread, drink black beer? Fie then! I much prefer a glass of wine to all their beer.

GRIMAUD

(still counting)

That's easy.

MOUSQUETON

If you please. You say it's easy?

GRIMAUD

(extending his hand towards the boat)

Port.

BLAISOIS

It is Port there in the barrels which we saw when Monsieur D'Artagnan opened the door?

GRIMAUD

Yes.

MOUSQUETON

Fine! But the door is closed. Ah—what a misfortune. Port is so fine.

GRIMAUD

The case!

MOUSQUETON

What, the case? Ah—yes the instrument case.

GRIMAUD

The screwdriver.

MOUSQUETON

Here.

(giving it to him. Grimaud puts it under the planks which form the closet)

What a man! What a man!

GRIMAUD

The drill!

BLAISOIS

Here it is.

GRIMAUD

The crowbar.

(Mousqueton passes him the crowbar)

Watch out.

(He raises the plank and enters into the compartment with the casks. Mousqueton and Blaisois stand watch)

(On the bridge.)

GROSLOW

I believe they are sleeping.

MORDAUNT

Do you still see their light?

GROSLOW

Yes, the little lantern in the cabin—but they're sleeping.

MORDAUNT

Then we must hasten. Your boat is ready—right?

GROSLOW

It is there. Do you see?

MORDAUNT

Where are we, then?

GROSLOW

On the Thames mouth.

MORDAUNT

Are there supplies in the boat and arms?

GROSLOW

Everything necessary.

MORDAUNT

You will stand ready with a cutlass for your men to cut the cord when we are embarked.

GROSLOW

I have my boarding axe.

MORDAUNT

There are still the servants of those wretches in the hold. Are they sleeping, too?

GROSLOW

We will see while passing their chamber to go into the boat.

MORDAUNT

Come on then—I'm in haste to finish.

(They descend.)

MOUSQUETON

(to Grimaud)

Well?

GRIMAUD

(with a cask)

Here goes.

MOUSQUETON

The cask is pierced.

GRIMAUD

It's up to the mark.

MOUSQUETON

What good luck.

BLAISOIS

Alarm! Someone's on his way down stairs—return.

MOUSQUETON

Ah my God! What will happen? There isn't time.

GRIMAUD

It's all right.

MOUSQUETON

This plank, quickly!

(The put the plank back where it was before. Grimaud hides behind the casks—the door opens.)

(Groslow and Mordaunt enveloped by their cloaks. Mordaunt holds a lantern.)

GROSLOW

What, not sleeping yet? It's contrary to the regulations.

MOUSQUETON

We were supping, gentlemen.

GROSLOW

Well, in ten minutes, the light will be extinguished and in a quarter of an hour be snoring!

MORDAUNT

(to Groslow)

Open the door, I beg you.

MOUSQUETON

Ah Lord Jesus! They're going to discover it.

BLAISOIS

Shall we warn our master?

(Groslow and Mordaunt go into the cabinet of casks and shut the door.)

MORDAUNT

(listening)

Yes, they sleep profoundly and God delivers them to me.

(Grimaud peeps from behind a cask)

Where are the full casks?

GROSLOW

This one here—and the two at the back. But here's where you can attach the wick. It has a tap.

MORDAUNT

(drawing a wick from his cape)

You say the wick lasts about eight minutes?

GROSLOW

Eight minutes.

MOUSQUETON

Can you hear what they are saying?

BLAISOIS

Not at all—only as they haven't yelled—they haven't found Grimaud.

MORDAUNT

And through this hole, which leads to the hold, I can light the wick without coming back in here.

GROSLOW

Perfectly! But don't rush. Wait till we are all embarked. The work is perilous—leave it to my second in command.

(Mordaunt attaches the wick to the cask.)

MORDAUNT

I do not entrust anyone with the execution of my vengeance. Don't worry yourself—when the clock strikes the quarter after—I will descend into the hold—you put your men in the boat, and at the moment warn me by a whistle.

GROSLOW

It will soon be done.

MORDAUNT

It will take me a minute to rejoin you—in one second, the cable is cut—we will row the oars vigorously—and soon—oh very soon— the frightening explosion—it will be a magnificent spectacle won't it, mother?

(takes off his hat and looks towards the sky)

GROSLOW

(recognizing Mordaunt)

Ah.

GROSLOW

I will run give the word to my men.

MORDAUNT

No—not a word, not a gesture—not the least noise. Don't awaken our enemies. You have a quarter of an hour—think of all that can happen in a quarter of an hour.

GROSLOW

No matter—don't waste time.

(they go to the door)

MOUSQUETON

I don't hear anything—did they kill him?

BLAISOIS

He would have cried. But they're opening the door—here they come.

GROSLOW

(after having locked the door)

Ah—my orders are followed. Go quick—quick

(to Mordaunt)

Go into the hold—I will go to the bridge.

MORDAUNT

A whistle—I set the fire.

(Hardly have they reshut the door when Grimaud, pale and trembling, rises. He holds the crowbar in his hands and goes to hit the
plank. The vessel commences to move.)

MOUSQUETON

(raising the plank)

Come, they're not here any more—well have you seen enough?

(He recommends silence to the lackeys and goes up to the Chamber
of the Musketeers.)

MOUSQUETON

Well, he's taking them wine?

(Grimaud is almost past the bridge. D'Artagnan makes a movement
and awakens.)

GRIMAUD

Hush!

D'ARTAGNAN

What is it?

GRIMAUD

Powder!

(whispering in his ear)

D'ARTAGNAN

Is it possible? My God!

(same action by Grimaud)

Horror!

(to Aramis—whispering in his ear)

Chevalier! Chevalier!

(he puts his hand on his shoulder)

Silence! Awaken, Athos.

(Aramis awakens Athos in the same way)

ATHOS

What's going on?

ARAMIS

Silence!

D'ARTAGNAN

(awakens Porthos who stands quickly and is about to speak when D'Artagnan closes his mouth)

Friends, friends—do you know who the Captain of this ship is? Colonel Groslow! Hush! Do you know what's in the casks of wine? Wait—

(he tears the cask from the hands of Grimaud and shows the powder)

Do you know who the man is who is going to fire that powder in a quarter of an hour? It's Mordaunt.

ATHOS

Mordaunt! We are lost!

ARAMIS

Protect us!

ATHOS

By God! Let's strangle them all!

D'ARTAGNAN

Silence—keep quiet. If Mordaunt sees he is discovered, he's capable of going down with us. Don't despair, we are not defenseless, we won't die. With enemies like Mr. Mordaunt, no mistakes—be sure of it—S'blood—Grimaud go bring your comrades up the little stairway—let's see....

(looking)

Have you confidence in me?

ALL

Oh! Speak! Speak!

D'ARTAGNAN

Well, there's only one role to take—no swords—no grand manners here. Let's leave.

PORTHOS

Leave—and which way?

D'ARTAGNAN

(opening the porthole from which one sees the sea)

Underneath this window is their long boat moored by a cable.

(looking)

Athos, Aramis, let's seize the cable, we will reach the long boat, we will cut the cord with your dagger and once isolated—on a sure terrain. Let them attack us if they dare. To the sea—to the sea.

(He attaches a cord ladder which descends to the sea.)

PORTHOS

It's going to be very cold.

D'ARTAGNAN

S'blood. It will be much too hot here rather soon. Our people are they here?

GRIMAUD, MOUSQUETON, BLAISOIS

Here we are!

BLAISOIS

I only know how to swim on my back.

PORTHOS

I'll take care of both of you.

(he grabs them by the waist)

D'ARTAGNAN

Let's go. Let's go.

(Athos descends the ladder—then Aramis. Then the others—the boat continues to move.)

GROSLOW

It is time—to the ladders quickly.

MEN'S VOICES

Here we are.

GROSLOW

Good! Are you holding the cable? Embark.

(he gives a whistle—the long boat disappears in the fog)

The cable is cut.

(One hears a great cry of despair from the wings—and one sees little by little the fire spread down the wick which Mordaunt has let from the hold.)

BLACKOUT

ACT V

Scene 12

Full sea. The ship has disappeared entirely. The theater represents the full sea lit by the moon. In the middle of the scene, the bark filled with seven men. Athos finishes cutting the cable with his dagger.

D'ARTAGNAN

Now, my friends, I believe that we are going to see something curious.

(One sees in the distance the little boat reappear with men on the bridge. The explosion follows—a bright light illuminates the sea.)

ARAMIS

It's superb!

PORTHOS

That's what it is!

D'ARTAGNAN

By this blow, we are relieved of that serpent. What do you think of it?

ATHOS

It's horrible! Horrible!

D'ARTAGNAN

Horrible if you like—but it's very consoling. Use our oars, my friends.

MORDAUNT

(In the sea)

Help me! Help!

D'ARTAGNAN

It's the voice of Mordaunt. Still with us, the demon!

MORDAUNT

(swimming)

Pity, gentlemen, pity in the name of heaven. I sense my strength fading.

ATHOS

The wretch. Stop, my friends.

D'ARTAGNAN

Athos, I tell you that if he gets within ten strokes of this ship I will split his head with an oar.

MORDAUNT

Grace, don't flee me, gentlemen. Grace—have pity for me.

ATHOS

Oh, this tears me apart! D'Artagnan—D'Artagnan—my son—he must live.

D'ARTAGNAN

S'blood, why not deliver yourself right away trussed up hands and feet to this wretch? That will soon be done.

MORDAUNT

Monsieur Comte de la Fère, it is you that I address. It is you that I beg. Have pity on me. Where are you, Monsieur Comte de la Fère— I don't see any more. I am dying. To me! To me!

ATHOS

(bending and extending his arms towards Mordaunt)

Here I am. Take my hand and enter our boat.

D'ARTAGNAN

I'd prefer not to see this. This weakness repulses me.

ATHOS

Well, put your other hand here.

(offering him his shoulder as a second point to lean on)

Now you are saved, be easy.

MORDAUNT

(with rage)

Ah—mother, I can offer you only one victim—but this will at least be the one you had chosen.

(D'Artagnan screams—Porthos raises an oar—Aramis looks for a place to strike. A push given the boat lands Athos in the water.)

PORTHOS

Oh Athos! Athos! Misfortune on us who let you die.

ARAMIS

Misfortune.

D'ARTAGNAN

Oh, yes, misfortune— Ah, see this body which rises slowly—it's

Mordaunt.

(One sees appear on the surface of the waves the cadaver of Mordaunt with the dagger in his heart.)

ARAMIS

He has a dagger in his heart.

PORTHOS

There he is, floating on the back of the waves.

D'ARTAGNAN

Ah! God's Blood! It's Mordaunt!

PORTHOS

Beautiful blow.

D'ARTAGNAN

But Athos, Athos—where is he?

(Athos reappearing and getting into the bark)

(Explosion of joy amongst the friends who lift Athos in.)

ARAMIS

Finally, God has spoken.

D'ARTAGNAN

Dead by the hand of Athos.

ATHOS

It wasn't I who killed him, it was destiny.

D'ARTAGNAN

What matter, provided he's dead and now friends—to France.

ALL

To France! To France!

CURTAIN

ABOUT FRANK J. MORLOCK

FRANK J. MORLOCK has written and translated many plays since retiring from the legal profession in 1992. His translations have also appeared on Project Gutenberg, the Alexandre Dumas Père web page, Literature in the Age of Napoléon, Infinite Artistries.com, and Munsey's (formerly Blackmask). In 2006 he received an award from the North American Jules Verne Society for his translations of Verne's plays. He lives and works in México.